The Author worked with an insurance broker with Lloyd's of London handling claims worldwide. On retirement he spent nigh on six years with two companies handling their claims.

BALADIN

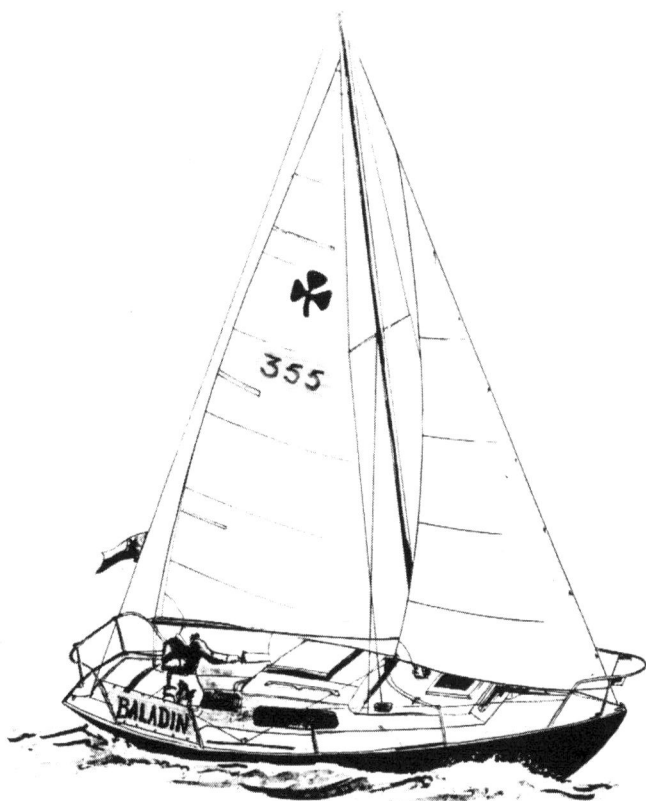

To my dear patient and tolerant wife Anne

Geoff Shelton

BALADIN

AUSTIN MACAULEY
PUBLISHERS LTD.

A CIP catalogue record for this title is available from the British Library.

ISBN 978 1 84963 571 4

www.austinmacauley.com

First Published (2014)
Austin Macauley Publishers Ltd.
25 Canada Square
Canary Wharf
London
E14 5LB

Printed and bound in Great Britain

Contents

1
The First Steps

There are many misguided people who think that purchasing a boat is as simple as buying a car or a washing machine, however nothing could be further from the truth. Buying a boat is not the product of divine inspiration nor indeed a fanciful whim. No sensible man awakes from his slumbers and announces 'Today I buy myself a boat'.

Most men with a spirit of adventure surging through their veins have fanciful dreams regarding the freedom of the seas, of snow white sails billowing with the fresh salt sea airs, with a warm sun percolating through one's clothes, the blue skies above and the gentle waves of green seas breaking into small white crests. For most these dreams lie dormant but for a minority the dream is constantly with you, niggling at the pit of your stomach, somewhere in your subconscious mind a voice is urging you to make that dream a reality.

No one can pin point with accuracy the very time they allowed themselves to be seduced with these flights of fancy. It could have been sparked off as a child on a visit to the seaside. It could have been a colourful travel brochure or a naval uniform. Interest may have been aroused by a film or a snatch of a seaman's conversation but you may be sure that whatever the cause the seed had been sown.

It may appear that from here on out that it was just a matter of making your purchase, but just as the dawn is slow to break so too is the proposed venture. There is of course the finance aspect. What can I afford? Where can I keep it? What are the running costs and indeed what type of boat? But dear reader there is one hurdle that can exceed and surpass all other considerations, namely one's spouse, one's very dear wife. From early in one's married state she has looked after you and cared for you. She has scrimped and saved for you, she has economised on your behalf and gone without. She has in your interest foregone new shoes, dresses and coats to ensure a happy and financially secure future. What would she say if she knew the thoughts rebounding in the caverns of your mind? It would be most unwise to tempt providence and reveal those plans, so our future sailor has to acquire subtlety. Already even in the absence of a vessel your character is being moulded without your being aware of it. Without a boat or a mooring, and even though the immediate prospect of acquiring those items may appear far off, you have got subtlety. The question is how to use it?

If a man knows his wife (which one suspects the majority do not) he will already be aware whether she is in favour, indifferent, opposed, violently opposed or would threaten divorce. Just as the seeds have been sown in your mind so you also must be the instigator of sowing seeds in your wife's mind. There are a variety of ways to do this and it may take years, but do not be disturbed by this, because you will slowly acquire another ingredient to your character, namely patience. This will be invaluable when you finally buy your boat.

While no aspiring sailor would openly admit the fact, but he is becoming devious. Subtlety is a better word but to oneself it is downright deviousness, for example buy a yachting magazine and when you get home claim it was given to you by a friend in the office. Never destroy the magazine, leave it lying around and even if you know where it is ask your wife if she has put it away somewhere. Do not at this stage mention buying a boat. By all means show her selective pictures and especially the ladies nautical fashions.

Make a habit of walking along towpaths and riverbanks or seashores. Linger at the sight of a boat whether you like it or not. Draw your wife's attention to its lines and shape, don't hesitate to express an opinion when the crew handling the vessel is older than yourself.

If you have children use them to advantage, take them on boating lakes, buy them toy yachts and motor boats. By indoctrinating your children they can without realising it speak to their mother of the joy they have experienced.

If you do not have children then buy yourself a small plastic boat that you can use in the bath. You may well be teased about this, but it is all part of the long term plan and every time your wife takes a bath your little boat will be there as a constant reminder, or to put it another way a constant advertisement.

It was the plastic tug boat that I bought for myself that finally worked the miracle, but in a manner that would not have my recommendation. It happened like this. My bathroom has blue tiled walls and one day when I had some central heating experts changing a radiator they did in the process chip one of the tiles. My wife rescued the china chippings and put them on the corner of the bath optimistically hoping that I would stick them back from whence they came. Some weeks elapsed without her hopes coming to fruition so being a tidy sort of person she put the blue and white chippings in my blue and white tug boat. The next time she put to sea (the boat not the wife) I was unaware she was carrying a dangerous deck cargo and when the aforesaid vessel hit rough waters she turned turtle and deposited her cargo in the vicinity of my backside. It was that episode and my lacerated posterior which caused me to think that a real boat could not be as dangerous as this, but how does one capitalise on such an event? Remember opportunities like this do not happen too often. The thing to do is to cry out loudly, make a fuss. Sure enough the better half came running and inspected the scene of the accident. After a brief conversation she uttered those magic words, words that I yearned to hear. "Well if you need a boat you had better get one."

"Do you really mean it?"

"Yes of course I do."

Now ladies frequently have a change of mind so it is necessary to tactfully remind them on appropriate occasions that your future boat has or will be bought with her blessing.

2
"Baladin"

The next stage is of course to find the right boat for you. I had in mind a nice 27 ft sloop with standing headroom and inboard diesel engine. No time should be lost, but one must not be panicked or sales talked into a vessel that does not appeal to you.

After months of looking at the lists of various yacht brochures I at last agreed to look at a 27 ft Halcyon lying in Heybridge basin, She appeared a little neglected what with everything inside being damp and smelling musty added to jars of jam with an inch of mould on the top, nevertheless I thought I could soon knock her into shape and made an offer.

That Saturday morning I arrived home and with smug satisfaction said to my wife, "I've found the boat I'm going to buy."

There was one of those pregnant pauses and then, "That's nice."

I tried to conceal the surge of joy that hammered within me but "That's nice" was not the response I had hoped for. I decided it would be preferable to keep a low profile. About twenty minutes later and again without looking up my wife said, "What happened about the gold watch you were going to buy me?" It is true I had been promising her one for over thirty years and if purchasing one now was some form of recompense for my getting a boat it was a good deal, but I was conscious I was on the defensive and didn't know how to rectify it.

So I said rather lamely, "I've only been waiting for you to make up your mind and I will be happy to buy you one."

There was no response but fifteen minutes later, "This toy of yours how much is it going to cost?" I told her.

The result was that I soon came to realise that I would have to modify my ambitions: something cheaper, something smaller, a little older with maybe an outboard engine and what does it matter if she doesn't have standing room.

The search began again, it took me over six months and then one day I saw this apparition of loveliness. She was standing on the hard on Wallasea Island down the River Crouch. She was a fin keel 21 ft Corribee and was blue and white just like my tug boat. Her name was BALADIN, she was absolutely exquisite and her lines, her contours it was unbelievable., I know now that love at first sight is true for I fell head over heels in love with her.

I cast my mind back home and suddenly realised that throughout the years when I had been carrying out this campaign for a boat, I had never told my wife what type of boat I was seeking; that had been stored and nurtured in the recesses of my mind and it is probable that while I had these grandiose ideas my wife had maybe been thinking of a 9 ft dinghy.

I made a successful offer for Baladin and suddenly I felt ten feet tall. I was now the Master of a real boat, the two of us would be a team, the world was ours for the taking. Little did I know then that Baladin had a will and a mind of her own; little did I know then that she would get me out of scrapes or act capriciously when I became over confident. I thought I could teach myself but Baladin had other ideas. She was the tutor and I the pupil.

Our base was to be the Essex Marina at Wallasea Island in the River Crouch.

3
The First Sail

I had been familiarising myself with the outboard, coming in and leaving the marina, also getting to grips with the sails and sheets, the kicking straps and the topping lift but as additional insurance I asked Derrick a colleague of mine who was an experienced sailor to join me. On the first Sunday in April we cast off but the outboard started to play up and for a few anxious moments Baladin refused to respond to the helm. There was a concerted effort by the other owners to assist, which appeared most noble but was probably due to them trying to protect their own investments. We, under the watchful eyes of our helpers exited the marina stern first and felt as though we were leaving an audience with the Queen as slowly we went our way.

Outside the marina we hoisted the sails. They looked bright in the sunshine as was to be expected in view of the previous owner having recently laundered them.

We headed into a fairly stiff easterly breeze though an ebbing tide gave us great assistance. The fact the tide was ebbing was purely coincidental. Using the tide to assist one's passage was still to me an unknown quantity. The area is of course known for its sand banks so I took the precaution of having the echo sounder on. We passed the mouth of the Roach and left Foulness Island to our starboard. Slowly we reached the open sea, this vast expanse of water as far as the eye could see. I switched off the echo sounder and we both laid back to wallow in this sheer luxury. A can of beer, a cheese roll and a pipe of strong tobacco, what else would a man want out of life?

As I idly watched the tobacco smoke passing over the stern I was interrupted by a noise from below. Almost in unison we said, "What was that?" It soon dawned on us that we had gone aground on the Ray Sands. We tried heeling her over to one side and using the engine but all to no avail. There were of course many things that could have been done but at the time they were unknown to me.

We lowered the anchor and waited and waited and waited. Slowly she keeled over and came to rest on the sands at a 45 degree angle. We climbed overboard put the anchor further out then walked over the sands. We managed to clean one side of the hull, meanwhile other yachtsmen were sailing up and down the Whittaker Channel which was no more than fifty yards away. I felt a bloody fool and suspected those grinning faces were echoing the same sentiments. I tried to give the impression as I cleaned the hull for the third time that I had intentionally beached BALADIN for that very purpose but I believe I was only fooling myself. Derrick had retired to the cabin and whilst lying at a rather uncomfortable angle read an old yachting magazine. It featured a cartoon from an April 1937 edition depicting a boat sitting on the mud. Its caption read "Think deeply, ye East Coast mud larkers."

At 17.30 the rising tide released us from the clutches below but alas not soon enough to ensure our arrival before dark.

Derrick was concerned at the lateness because his wife was unaware of where the boat was berthed or even what its name was. I was concerned because I had no battery aboard for navigation lights. All I could do was to light the paraffin lamp in the cabin and pull back the curtains. At least we could be seen from the side.

At 21.30 we arrived back in the marina and after waving Derrick goodbye I turned over in my mind the events of the day. I had made mistakes but with it came knowledge. I would never take depth for granted again, I would never go aground again. Baladin excelled herself, we will work in harmony, we'll be a team, we'll explore the rivers and creeks, we'll go up the coast and down the coast we'll go yes by jingo one day we'll go to a foreign country, but just for now steady as she goes.

Derrick never did come sailing with me again.

4

Away Outboard

There is so much one can learn from a book but equally as much can be forgotten, there is however nothing like a practical experience to indelibly etch on one's mind the constant need to be aware of tides and winds and your relative position in the scheme of the elements.

One Sunday morning with glorious sunshine and a slight breeze Baladin and I decided to explore the upper reaches of the Crouch. In the cockpit was a supply of food and drink so there was no necessity to leave the tiller except for the adjustments to the sails.

At this stage in my nautical education I was not noticeably conscious of the tides, after all I was only going up stream. It was purely coincidental that the tide happened to be with me at the start, but it soon changed and the ebb slowed down my progress. This did not worry me, time was unimportant and I was out to enjoy a quiet peaceful and tranquil sail.

Sometime in the late afternoon I decided to return but of course the tide had also turned again but now I had this light breeze against me. Tacking back and forth across the river I was grabbing about 50 yards at a time. This was not unpleasant except it was now only an hour before dark so I decided to motor back. I started the outboard, dropped the jib and then went amidships to drop the main. It was while standing on the cabin hatch that I heard the engine race and as I looked aft I was just in time to see the outboard leap into the air and disappear over the side, The wooden bracket to which it was attached and which was about 1½ inches thick was snapped in two, the missing half being still attached to the engine somewhere in the mud below me. There was no time to think about the cause, for I had to concentrate on hoisting the sails again. I could of course have dropped the anchor whilst I sorted myself out, or waited for the tide to change, but that did not occur to me. I was set on getting back to the marina that night. The current had already carried me some considerable distance upstream so I had to make that up at 50 yards a time. The marina was barely two miles away and now that it was dark I could see the arc light of a timber ship which was being unloaded at the wharf. Alas I had no battery aboard for my navigation lights, not having planned to be out after dark, it was inconceivable that I should still be out so late but in reality I was.

About 23.00 I could hear the deep throb of engines approaching but no navigation lights could be seen. What bloody fool would be out on the water at this time of night without navigation lights? What bloody fool indeed. I called out as loudly as I could, "Ahoy there, ahoy there." I never did see that vessel but from the conversation we exchanged through the dark night air I gleaned it was an ex-torpedo boat which had been stuck on the Ray Sands. The crew were due to meet their wives at 21.00 in the Wardroom but alas it was now closed.

About 23.30 I tied up in the marina and then fell flat on my face on the pontoon.

Now I had time to think. What went wrong, what did I do that was wrong? Alas there were many things but the main fault was the spot I had chosen to take the sails down. Had I done this mid-stream then the current would have carried me upstream. The spot I had chosen was just off Bridgemarsh Island. With the engine in neutral and being too near the bank the current had taken Baladin stern first into a mudbank thereby forcing the engine under then up until the strain broke the bracket.

I learnt a lot that day but apart from acquiring knowledge in this expensive manner I have a sneaking feeling that Baladin objects to the engine hanging over her stern, for she is very conscious that it detracts from her appearance but she doesn't have to be a party to such a drastic course of action.

5
First Rally

The Corribee Owners Association had organised a rally at Brightlingsea to which I had been invited. This was to be my first challenge that would take me out to sea. I bought the necessary charts and studied the tides. After plotting my course I prepared for the voyage having stocked up with food, beer and tobacco and plenty of water. As I cast off from the marina I could not but help reflect that the last time I went to sea I mean really to sea, ropes were made of hemp or jute, there were grass lines and tarred spun yarn, sails were made of canvas and boats were made of wood. Each ingredient had its own particular aroma. No boats were made in those days of glass reinforced plastic. In fact I doubt whether it had been invented. They had nylon but whenever anyone spoke of nylon they thought in terms of ladies stockings (tights had not been thought of either) but I digress, Baladin with all these newfangled inventions and I set out on the ebb tide, the sun was warm and just a light breeze accompanied us.

I was barely out of the Crouch when a sea mist descended which reduced visibility to two hundred yards. I kept to my compass course and wallowed in a smug sense of self-congratulation as each buoy came into view just where it and indeed we should be. Then I experienced my first problem. The next buoy in the Whittaker Channel should have been the Ridge but it wasn't, it was the South Buxey. Never mind I could easily have missed the Ridge in the mist, I knew at the South Buxey I had to change course to starboard to miss the sands on the port side and then come back in again. I duly did this until suddenly I came to the Ridge. What the hell had happened? I checked my charts and everything was shown thereon exactly as I had plotted it: it must have been my compass thatwas at fault and if so then I had no idea where I was. What the hell I'll just let the wind and tide take me wheresoever it wishes. In actual fact I decided to follow the tide out to sea but with the aid of the echo sounder I hugged the sand banks to keep me out of the shipping channel. The wind freshened and the mists cleared. Now I could see land but apart from supposing I was off Clacton I had no idea where I was. The thing to do was to change to a westerly course and maybe drop anchor off Mersea island or wherever I happened to end up. Suddenly a buoy came into view and on closer inspection I found it was the Colne Bar. This was fantastic, this was the entrance to the Colne which would lead me to Brightlingsea. Good old Baladin she doesn't say much but she knows what she's doing.

Arriving in Brightlingsea I was met by Colin who was organising the rally and tied up alongside his boat "Roaring Forties".

Having told Colin of the problem I had experienced he said let me see your chart. He turned it over and there attached to the back was a notice to mariners showing that the authorities had reversed the Ridge and South Buxey buoys. This meant that when I altered course to avoid the Buxey sands I had in fact gone over the Foulness sands without realising it, and so another lesson had been learnt.

That evening Colin and I adjourned to the Colne Yacht Club where we enjoyed a convivial evening. At 23.00 we left and Colin suggested that as I did not have a tender I should use his and he would collect it in the morning. Baladin was of course tied to the poles in mid-stream. To acquaint me with his 2 HP outboard we set out from the jetty, covered a hundred yards and returned. Now Colin is quite a big fellow and with my 17 stone we were quite low in the water. Colin was amidships and I was in the stern. As he stepped upon the jetty the dinghy's bows rose and the transom was therefore barely four inches above the water.

"I should sit in the centre," said Colin.

"No it's alright," I replied and with a parting wave set out into the inky darkness of the night. Colin waited on the jetty, and although he could not see me he could hear the engine and therefore knew whether I had safely reached Baladin.

About a hundred yards out the dinghy just turned upside down, a small wave having come over the stern, I found the painter and started to swim on my back towing the upturned boat. I then heard Colin's voice coming out of the night, "Are you alright?"

"Yes," I called back.

"Has the engine cut out?"

"Not exactly, the boat's upside down." Eventually I got to the jetty. Colin made a move to pull me out but I said, "Get the boat first."

"To hell with the dinghy," he replied which prompted a response from me

"I haven't towed it all this way for you to abandon it now." Colin pulled the boat onto the jetty, but then he couldn't pull me out, however assistance from a passing sailor resolved that problem, though; with green slime all over me I wasn't a pretty sight.

It was gone midnight when I eventually boarded Baladin.

I had intended returning home on the Sunday, but the wind was blowing hard and Colin and Malcolm (who also has a Corribee named "Beatrice") advised me not to go especially on my own, but I was quite adamant. In retrospect they were both right, but I was too green to appreciate it then, anyway Malcolm said he would come with me. We reefed the main and wore a storm jib. Malcolm's preparation was calm and efficient and I made a mental note to follow his example on any future voyage.

We took the ebb tide and with the wind blowing force 4/5 from the S.W. we just seemed to take off. Malcolm did not have any wet gear with him, so he had the bottom half of mine and I had the top. That way we both got soaked to the skin. We returned the same way I had come by going through the Swin but once in the Whittaker Channel the wind was on the nose and there was still two hours of the ebb tide left. Visibility was poor and frankly we just had the hell knocked out of us. I fell against the echo sounder and broke the support and then when I leant over the stern to start the engine to assist us I lost my pocket compass overboard. The jib sheet got caught round a cleat on the mast so I tied myself to the boat and crawled forward to release it, then the shackle pin came out of the jib and Malcolm insisted on rectifying it.

It took us over eight hours to get back to Wallasea and we were both cold, wet and exhausted, but after a change into dry clothes and a bowl of hot soup our spirits were soon restored. Not only did I learn from Malcolm but confidence in Baladin was increasing by leaps and bounds.

6
Laying Up

The Corribee Owners Association hold a laying up lunch each year but I have always suspected the motive. Is it for example a form of harvest thanksgiving for a successful sailing season or is it a "wake" while boat and owner hibernate. Whatever the reasons may be I find the laying up period disruptive and miserable and lonely.

They took Baladin out of the water this year; in fact they did it a week earlier than instructed which in itself was a bad omen. Imagine going down to the marina for the last sail of the year and finding your boat missing. Once over the initial shock, you find her on the hard with the mast down, rigging in a total state of disorder and a couple of rusting oil cans supporting her either side, wedged in with odd bits of timber. I felt depressed and sad for Baladin. It was so undignified and not befitting to such a graceful lady. I did my best to reassure her that she would not be neglected and that the period would be used profitably in her interests.

Intentions can be noble as I hoped mine were, but circumstances frequently decree they be modified. I'm afraid this was the case here. First of all they had put Baladin on the north side of some huge monster which kept the sun away. This meant that the woodwork was not given a chance to dry out in preparation for treatment, then it was either too cold or too windy, or there was snow, ice and frosts, but every Sunday I faithfully went down to see her. The owners of the other boats were absent and the public house almost deserted. It is possible that you may be thinking, "Why then does he go?"

The answer is simply that my wife was so schooled into my not being home of a Sunday that it was easier to maintain my disappearance every week than to have to re-educate her in the spring. Believe me the sacrifice was mine. While I was sitting in a cold cabin eating cheese and biscuits for my

Sunday lunch, my mind would drift back home where I had witnessed the preparations of the joint and vegetables. In a moment of weakness I would rush down to the pub for a hot soup and hamburger, only to be informed that there was no call for such a thing at this time of the year.

Slowly Baladin became dirtier and dirtier, and then to add insult to injury they put on the other side of her a small neglected little boat. She looked as though she had been abandoned, her wash boards were broken, her dodgers torn, her woodwork was water scarred with years of neglect, her rubbing strake was broken and everything was covered in green algae. How could anyone do this, she deserved so much better. In a moment of madness I thought I would adopt her but Baladin soon put those ideas out of my head. There is no way she would tolerate a competitor.

The weeks passed into months and the work progressed very slowly. I assured Baladin that she would be the first to go back into the water and that I would personally accompany her, and so she was and I did.

Back in her natural environment she was happy, all her bits and pieces were now in the right places and she welcomed the small refinements that enhanced her appearance. I have however made her a promise, that I will not take her out of the water next year, and in return (although she is as yet unaware of it) she will allow me to enjoy a Sunday lunch.

7
It's Not Cricket – by "Baladin"

I was on the verge of relating the following event, when Baladin insisted that she was in a far better position to portray the truth than I was, so I will sit back and let her take over.

BY BALADIN

The following event is a true and accurate account of an incident to which I would have preferred not to be a party, however, I have heard so many versions of this event, each of which strays from the truth, that I felt as the only impartial witness in attendance that it was beholden upon me to set the record straight.

Where better to start this story than at the beginning. Imagine if you will a glorious summer day. I am lying in my berth at Wallasea Marina with the gentle sound of the water lapping around my hull. At the same time the Master (it satisfies his ego to be called that so excuse me if I indulge him) was ten miles away attending a cricket match sponsored by the company that employs him. The hospitality tent had rather more attention by some characters than had the cricket, however toward late afternoon the liquid refreshments began to have a marked effect.

Now that you have the picture let me introduce you to the villains. First we have Howard, long, lean, lanky and raucous, then you have Hugh, long, far from lean and a brewers goitre meant he most decidedly was not lanky. Suddenly as Big Hugh's bulk made his way through the crowd he was heard to roar out repeatedly, "Who's coming out on Shelton's ship." The Master was quick to sum up the situation and decided (to avoid embarrassment to the other guests) to bring these villains down to see me. On the way Big Hugh bought a bottle of whisky which by all accounts was unnecessary for the reason he already had liquor up to the gills and secondly from the beer cans that keep popping open it is apparent that the Master has an adequate supply.

My first knowledge of this impending boarding party was when I heard Big Hugh calling out ribald comments to courting couples on the sea wall.

I sank a little as all three came aboard but the Master soon had the engine working and the sails ready for hoisting.

With anybody else aboard this could have been a delightful evening's sail. It all appeared peaceful aboard if of course one accepts that all three were being most rude to each other however Howard had already been at the whisky and handed to the Master a plastic beaker half full. At the same time Big Hugh emerged from the cabin wearing swimming trunks. Now the Master thought he was going to sunbathe. Never for one moment did he think that while under full sail Big Hugh would dive overboard, but he did. I say dive but it was a belly flop and with Big Hugh's large belly there was some splash, to the extent that it not only soaked the Master but filled his beaker with salt water. This episode did not endear Big Hugh to the Master especially as the blend of whisky was not something you would recommend.

The next thing is that Howard emerges from the cabin with a pair of the Master's swimming shorts. How he kept them on is a mystery, because the Master is almost but not quite as large as Big Hugh. Howard of course went overboard.

Now I happen to know that the Master is inexperienced in picking bodies out of the sea, and especially is this so under sail.

Time passed by and it was ready for them to come inboard. I must confess I had always thought such an evolution would be easy but it didn't work. Big Hugh put his hands on the port side expecting to spring aboard but the only thing that happened was I leaned over under his weight. Howard then tried but also without success. Howard then conceived the idea of diving under Big Hugh and putting his head under Big Hugh's backside it would have the right effect. The very idea is revolting to the extreme, but the end result was failure on the one hand and Howard gasping for air on the other.

Needless to say the tide was carrying us onto a sandbank so the Master had to start up the engine and tow them into mid-stream. He then prepared a rope, tied loops in it and hung that over my stern. Both swimmers failed in their endeavours and fell back into the water hysterical with laughter. The Master was unaware whether it was the liquor that was causing the hilarity or the infectiousness of the parties to the futility of the circumstances they were confronted with. Either way the Master was€ getting worried and he could already see tomorrow's headlines: "Cricket guests drowned at sea" or "Firm sacks staff for drowning their guests". Meanwhile I was drifting again so further remedial action was necessary.

The Master then had a flash of brilliance. Over my stern locker is a grating with four horizontal slats. He took it off, tied a rope to two corners and hung it over the side to be used as a ladder. At long last we got Howard on board but Big Hugh just could not manipulate the grating to his advantage. He then suggested to the Master that he should tow him back to the marina. My immediate reaction was how undignified. I would look like a whaling ship towing a whale, the Master however was now getting irate. "I'm not towing you back five miles now get aboard this !X?X!! ship."

I've never heard him let off like this before but gathered he was indeed very worried.

He then put a rope on each corner of the grating, tied the ends to the main sheet halyard wound it round the winch told him in no uncertain terms to stand on the grating then proceeded with Howard's assistance to winch him inboard.

Over an hour had passed since starting this exercise and dusk was setting in. The sails were taken down and we proceeded back under power meanwhile Big Hugh had discarded his trunks and stood naked in the cabin hatch with some whisky.

Now under normal circumstances this would have been alright though mark you it wasn't a pleasant sight but somehow the whisky went down the wrong way with the result that Big Hugh spat it all into the wind. That in itself was sacrilege but to do it into the wind especially when the Master was sitting down wind evoked another stream of expletives.

The next thing of course was the shame I felt as we passed The Royal Corinthian Yacht Club for the reason that this motley crew were singing sea shanties but using the lyrics from some coarse rugby songs.

At last we arrived back in the marina but no sooner had we tied up when Big Hugh decided he wanted a dry shirt. The shirt of course was in the car as also were the keys.

Big Hugh borrowed a wire coat hanger and departed down the pontoons. It is now nearly 2100 and Big Hugh is working on his car when the security man arrives with two Alsatian dogs.

"What are you doing sir?"

"What the hell does it look like?"

"Is that your car?"

"Of course it is."

"I see sir what are you doing down here?"

"I've been sailing."

"What's the name of your boat?"

"I haven't got one, it's a mate's."

"I see sir and what is the name of it?"

"How the hell should I know!"

This was a surprising statement when Big Hugh had been swimming around me for over an hour and my name is blazoned in letters over a foot high on either side.

The security man left while Big Hugh inflicted over £60 of damage to his car. When he at last succeeded in his endeavours he returned to the berth where he was optimistic enough to believe he could have some more of his own whisky, however Howard and the Master had deprived him of that little indulgence though he could of course have smelled the empty bottle. The result was another stream of expletives.

At last they departed into the night leaving me to return to peace and tranquillity, and to ponder on how any of them could distort and embroider such a simple story, oh yes and by the way we never did get the wire coat hanger back.

8
Winter Sailing

The fields and hedgerows of the Essex countryside were rimed with a February hoar frost. Dawn had not yet broken and the car's headlights had picked up a variety of nocturnal creatures scurrying out of the way. Inside the car it was warm and one felt insulated against harsh elements outside.

Fleeting thoughts passed through my mind which cast doubt on my sanity for leaving a warm bed and warm house to embark on such a mission, but almost immediately I cast those thoughts aside knowing I was already committed.

I wondered how I came to be in this situation and quietly reflected on the telephone call the previous Wednesday. It was Howard to inform me that he was moving his boat, a Caravelle named "Sea Breeze", from the marina at Wallasea on The Crouch to Heybridge Basin on The Blackwater. Would I accompany him? I said "Yes" before he had finished, and then I immediately thought that it would be prudent to speak to my wife first. I suggested he hold on until I had spoken to my better half. Her response was "You know you're going whatever I say, so why ask?"

0730 on Saturday morning was to be our departure time, so that is how I came to be travelling through the Essex marshes at such an early hour.

Walking along the sea wall a slight breeze stung my face and even though it was weak it seemed to penetrate every article of clothing. The frost was so thick that it looked like a thin coating of snow. There was no sign of life except a set of footprints on the pontoons from which I gathered that Howard was up and about and had already visited the showers. Suddenly I noticed that nearly all the boats were stuck on the mud. I realised we were on springs but I had never seen it go out this far before. Howard's tousled head appeared out of the cabin bemoaning the fact that our departure would now be delayed by two hours and that his engine was not strong enough to make headway against the incoming tide. My own outboard was at home following its winter service so I offered to go and pick it up.

My arrival home found my dear wife sitting up in bed watching morning television, with a steaming cup of coffee and hot buttered toast. Wives have been given a special gift denied to us men; they are telepathic, they are thought readers. "You must be mad." I gave a sickly grin and departed post haste before I was tempted to leave Howard more high and dry than he already was.

At last we were able to cast off. We passed Baladin and though I gave her a backward glance I hoped that she had not seen me consorting with another boat. She would not have approved.

The sky was a pale clear blue, the sun was shining but without warmth and the wind was just a light breeze. With both engines going we punched the tide and made good time, which was necessary as we were going to take the short cut over the Ray Sands. We hoisted the sails, cut the engines and took advantage of a slightly stronger S.E. wind. We both felt sluggish as every action was an effort; our feet and hands were frozen, and everything we touched appeared cold and wet.

A mist descended which denied us the benefit of coastal fixes, nevertheless we hopped from buoy to buoy and really enjoyed the sail. No other boats were to be seen and a slow realisation came over us that we were the only sane people about. How could people deny themselves the pleasure that we were now experiencing? Had our feet and hands been able to express an opinion they would no doubt have taken a contrary view.

We opened a flask of hot soup followed by sausage rolls. Howard then brought out some cans of beer but I reluctantly declined for the simple reason that in this weather it goes right through and I had no desire to expose any part of my anatomy that wasn't vitally necessary and that is presupposing I could have found my way through various layers of clothing.

At long last we entered the Colne and with it Brightlingsea which was to be our overnight stay. Howard was not only Skipper and navigator but Galley Slave too, and it was not long before we both read and re-read the instructions on tins, the contents of which still remain a mystery, but suffice to say our meal was steaming hot, palatable, filling and appetising.

We were tied up against the poles mid-stream and went ashore to the Colne Yacht Club which is really the most hospitable club I've met, but regrettably the shower room was closed until Sunday morning. Howard was disappointed, but psychologically I was somewhat relieved, it was too cold to strip off, and in any case there is always the feeling that a layer of dirt is a further layer of insulation.

We strolled round town and then adjourned to the "Yachtsman's Arms" where we slowly thawed out. After some considerable time and a fair intake of the local brew our cheeks began to burn with the warmth. A smoky, fuggy atmosphere permeated through the haze thereby allowing us to take aim at the dartboard. At 2300 we reluctantly bade the landlord farewell and made our way down to the slipway to take the dinghy back to "Sea Breeze". Our liquid intake acted like an immersion heater, we were not cold only aware of it.

As soon as we arrived on board we prepared to turn in. Howard had the forward cabin while I had the starboard bunk in the main cabin. I removed the minimum of clothing then I found I could not easily turn and then nature called I got back into the creaking bunk and the zip on my sleeping bag jammed then nature called. I had no sooner remedied the problem and nature called.

I turned the sleeping bag round the other way so that my head was aft. Strong gusts of icy wind found the gaps in the washboards and went straight down my neck. I pulled the bag over my head but then when I stretched my legs my head came out and nature called.

Snores from the forward cabin told me Howard was not having similar problems. I lay on my back unable to turn left or right regretting that I had consumed so much but hoping I was now empty, but I wasn't. Shafts of Arctic weather streaking through the hatch left me with neuralgic head pains. I did not get any sleep that night but in that unexplainable mysterious plan of life some good came out of the experience. You see Howard and Sue have a loveable dog called Motty but in spite of his delightful nature they had noticed that when sleeping aboard he usually awoke suffering from rheumatic pains and was far from cheerful.

When relating my nights experience to Howard he said, "Well that explains everything. You slept in Motty's bunk," so in retrospect I was to achieve a form of communication denied to Motty thereby ensuring his future draft free nights.

At 0930 on Sunday morning we slipped our moorings. The winds of the night had dropped but it was still a force 5 from the S.E. The sky was full of low dark clouds scudding menacingly above us. Visibility was about four miles and it was just as cold.

We sailed down the River Colne giving the Mersea flats a wide berth. We cut across Bench Head to the Bench Head buoy and entered the River Blackwater. The menacing looking power station at Bradwell looked dark and forbidding, while just opposite moored fore and aft were a number of merchant vessels which had been laid up. The RNLI inshore lifeboat went scurrying by and we hoped no fellow sailors were in trouble. If there is a day to be in difficulty this is not lt.

The Lockgates at Heybridge opened at high tide which was 1330. We arrived at 1300 and saw Sue and Motty waiting to greet us. After tying up outside the lock gates we headed for the local tavern with its plentiful supply of hot food. Meanwhile the Lock Keeper had very kindly said he would give us a call when it was time to open the gates.

Sue and Motty joined us aboard, but as we came out of the lock we were confronted with the canal which was frozen over. Fortunately the ice was not thick and did not therefore impede our progress to "Sea Breeze" winter berth.

In spite of the cold and privations it was a great weekend, a valuable experience and one that I would be happy to repeat.

9

"Charlie"

Brightlingsea is a popular place for the Corribee Owners Association to hold its East Coast Rally so once again I set sail from the Crouch.

I left at 0545 in a force 4 gusting 5 from the S.W. and an ebbing tide. Constant rain squalls did not prevent us from averaging over 5 knots. I went through the Spitway and took advantage of the tide which had now turned, the seas however took on a different character with a strong side wind. White crests extended as far as the eye could see and Baladin was taking a bit of a hammering, but we made good time arriving in Brightlingsea in Just under four and half hours.

On the Saturday morning Colin aboard "Roaring Forties" with his son James decided to join me and the two boats would then go and meet Bob and Pat aboard "Snowball" who were coming from the back of Mersea Island.

We entered the Colne and proceeded downstream against the tide. Now moored in the river were some cargo boats one of which was a Swedish ship called "Charlie". Why a Swedish ship should be called Charlie I have never been able to fathom out, but its name and port of origin are irrelevant to what transpired, all that is important is that Charlie was anchored mid-stream. Colin decided to go up the lee side, and to steal a march on Colin I decided to go up the windward side. Before I had a chance to congratulate myself on my so called smart move, the wind suddenly stopped, the sails went limp, the current took control and before I could do anything Baladin had rammed the monster at right angles.

Suddenly I heard the sound of feet climbing metal companion ways and running across steel decks, and in no time at all there was the skipper and his crew looking down at me.

"Vot you doing to my ship?" yelled the skipper.

"Sorry," I called, "but steam gives way to sail."

With visible disbelief he said, "But I am at anchor."

"That's no excuse," I cried.

This brief conversation was carried out with Baladin still drifting out of control down its starboard side and the crew above walking aft as they followed our progress.

Baladin however had taken exception to this foreign vessel being in our way, and like a young terrier she was determined to have another go. The opportunity came sooner than expected. Over "Charlie's" stern was a huge green oil drum into which they put their garbage, Baladin's cross trees caught it with the result that its contents poured out over the foredeck and the genoa. Shrieks of laughter broke out from above meanwhile with the wind now filling the sails Baladin with an air of disdain took off up the lee side.

The trip home was even rougher than going to Brightlingsea. I cast off at 1105. It took me nearly three hours to get to the Bench Head, and another 40 minutes to the Eagle. I changed course to 220 degrees to cross the Ray Sands. High Tide was still an hour away but one cannot afford to make mistakes in this area.

I complimented the sails with the engine but even then the seas constantly knocked us off course. My glasses were so rimed with salt that I could not see through them and without them I could not read my chart or easily see the buoys, but the aerial masts on Foulness (there are three of them) I could see and within a degree of my plotted course, they proved very acceptable and a fantastic aid to navigation. Entering the Crouch on an ebb tide and a S.W. wind I decided to keep the engine going. Ahead of us was a large sixty foot vessel covered in canvas and with a large crew scurrying about her decks. Whether she was a training ship or not I do not know but Baladin caught and passed her with ease. The skipper gave me a dirty look as I overtook them but in fairness I don't think he was aware my engine was running.

At 1800 I tied up in the marina with the sun shining and barely a ripple on the water. It had taken me nearly seven hours to do the short route over the sands as opposed to four and a half hours for the outward passage going the long way.

This merely enforced the lesson I had already learnt of the value of using the tides to one's advantage.

10
Baladin Abroad

It was inevitable that sooner or later Baladin and I would cross the Channel together. Our courtship had lasted some considerable time now and it was timely that we should embark on something a little more challenging. My confidence in Baladin's ability had grown and my affection had not diminished. I do not think this was reciprocated, but I believe she feels that she must indulge an old man with his flights of fancy and be there to hold his hand when he gets into trouble.

Baladin would like to take credit for the idea of a channel crossing but in reality she had overheard Howard and Sue discussing it with me and it was they who suggested that Baladin and Sea Breeze might enjoy each other's company on such a venture, and so on the 21st July Howard in Sea Breeze set out from the Blackwater and Baladin and I from Wallasea Island.

We had decided that we would spend the first night in the River Swale behind the Isle of Sheppey. My wife had advised me not to endanger the lives of anybody else's son, husband or father. She did not mention daughters but I got the message and went solo.

Unfortunately I do not have any devices such as self-steering auto helms, roller reefing or radio so once at the tiller you stay there until you reach your destination, and so on this first day with very light winds it took me 12 hours. Sea Breeze overtook me and being a faster boat arrived at least an hour before me, but Baladin will not be rushed. With her nose in the air she acts like a gracious and elegant young lady which of course is what she is.

On the Sunday we left for Ramsgate. The seas were a little lumpy, but I must have done something to upset Baladin because she appeared to be in a petulant mood. If I lose concentration she'll clout me with the boom or suddenly spin round or cause me to get an unexpected soaking. I experienced all this during the day with the result that in my attempts to counteract her capricious behaviour the strain caused the seam of my trousers to go and then again and again with the result that it was only the zip that was holding the two legs together.

Howard could not understand where we had got to, he having been tied up in Ramsgate for two hours so he enquired of a recent arrival whether he had spotted us.

"Yes," he said, "he's just outside the harbour but all I saw was his legs in the air."

In reality I had slipped in the cockpit well, got jammed under the tiller (you can do that with 17 stone) with both legs in the air and convulsed with laughter, meanwhile Baladin was doing a ballet dance. Conditions outside the harbour were very rough and especially so when one has to leave the tiller to go forward and take down the jib, and then of course there was the embarrassment of entering the harbour. The sea walls either side have their usual quota of sightseers looking down at you, while I'm sitting there with crossed legs in a forlorn attempt to conceal the fact that my trousers have seen better days.

Weather conditions confined us to Ramsgate for a few days but eventually the day dawned with north winds force 3/4 locally 5. With the wind on our port beam we set off but not before making an arrangement that if either boat was in trouble we would jiggle our jib. Now many of you may know that in the channel there are three shipping lanes. Each has to be crossed at right angles and there is a minimum speed of 4 knots to be maintained. So as Dunkerque was our destination and it was forty miles away the passage should take ten hours.

The course was to be via the North Goodwin Lightship then to Mid Falls a red can buoy which is on the edge of the first shipping lane. Sea Breeze was far ahead at this stage so I started the engine to make certain that I was maintaining the regulation minimum speed. I do not carry a log but if you check your distances between the buoys carefully as shown on your chart, you can calculate in advance your estimated time of arrival based on four knots. If you are behind time then start the engine, for failing to do so not only offends the people who make the rules but it also upsets all your pre-arranged navigational exercises which are based on your achieving an average of four knots, and of course being single handed you cannot just drop everything and start replotting your course.

Everything appeared to be going well until in the middle of the first shipping lane the engine cut out. Try as I might she would not go. I jiggled my jib but Sea Breeze was too far ahead to see it. A decision had to be taken: do I go on, or do I go back? I should explain here if I have not already done so but Baladin dislikes the outboard. She thinks it spoils her good looks, which of course it does, and she also thinks it is a reflection on her own capabilities as though I lack total confidence in her. I then thought "should I be worried" and the answer came back "No". The time to worry is entering harbour whether it be Ramsgate or Dunkerque. I then spoke to Baladin, "Come on old girl it's just you and me, now show us what you can do." I don't think she approved of the "old girl" expression but she took off like a young gazelle. Regrettably only a 3 knot gazelle, but she stuck her nose into the seas eastward bound.

A freak wave caught us on the port beam, hit me in the back and knocked me into the cockpit well, but that apart we progressed slowly. My charted course was now incorrect and the tide in the Dunkerque Road was against me, with the result that I had drifted down to Dunkerque West rather than East. The allotted ten hours had now passed but I still had five miles to go against the tide and with very little wind.

Near the entrance to Dunkerque East another sailor recognising that I was having difficulties called over. Regrettably we neither spoke the other's language but he indicated he would see me in. Once in the harbour's entrance I took down the main and just left the jib. It was now getting dark and Sue and Howard and I had promised to open a bottle of champagne to celebrate our arrival. They had not taken account of my slow progress or misfortune but back to Baladin, she very slowly and graciously went up the canal to the yacht marina; she went in, found an empty berth and slotted in so nicely she barely touched the pontoon. She had excelled herself, she had made her point. Now the yacht marina in Dunkerque is split between two clubs. I had to take pot luck where I went which happened to be the one furthest from the Club House.

Howard and Sue meanwhile were in the Club House when news reached them of my arrival some 4 to 5 hours later than expected. Howard got into his dinghy and came over to see me. It was only then that I realised that the part of the marina I was in was locked so the only exit was by Howard's dinghy. We made the Club House just before they closed but not before Howard and Sue had bought me a huge bacon sandwich with chips and a pint of beer. I have never tasted anything so enjoyable in my life, you can keep the champagne I'll take the beer. We retired to our respective vessels exceedingly tired but with a smug sense of self-satisfaction.

The following morning I swung my legs out of the bunk and was horrified to see they had turned yellow. I didn't feel ill but anyone with yellow legs should feel ill. What does one do with yellow legs, they didn't hurt, they weren't sore, seems a little silly to call a doctor when you feel well and all you've got is yellow legs, and again how do you tell a French doctor you've got yellow legs. "Doctor je suis yellow legs!" While contemplating my next move I decided to make a cup of tea. In the process of pouring water into the kettle some ran over my legs and left in its wake a pink mark. I took the flannel and washed both legs and restored them to their original condition, apparently the dye had come off my sleeping bag.

I acquired a spare part for the engine something to do with the lead to the sparking plug. Not being mechanically minded it worked and though I found a certain comfort in having the engine back Baladin was not too pleased in fact you somehow sensed that she'd get her own back somehow.

The following day we were heading for Ostend. The forecast was 4 to 5 locally 6. It appeared that we were in for a rough passage but in reality it never went beyond 3. It took us four and a half hours to make the passage and when we got there it was unbelievably overcrowded. We did not "lock in" to the main yacht basin but stayed outside tucked inside the harbour wall. This allowed those vessels to leave at will, but it also meant you were rafted together with as many as six boats. Being the smallest I was always on the outside so I didn't have other crews crawling all over me.

The next day I awoke early sensing there would be plenty of activity and went ashore for fuel. On my return I found the two innermost boats wanted to get out so I decided I may as well depart at the same time. The anxiousness of the two inner boats rather rushed me into casting off before I had checked all my gear. I had got into the habit of checking the shackles and bottle screws and all the sheets and moving parts before I left harbour. This day I didn't with the result that in the rush I had forgotten to remove the expanding strap that I use to stop the running rigging making a noise.

Outside the harbour I had endeavoured to hoist the main only to get the thing caught up in the strap. I could not raise it, I could not lower it. Baladin was wallowing all over the place. Somehow with the aid of the telescopic boat hook I managed to free it, but as I did so a baton flew out of the sail, I fell backwards landing on the quick release to the mainsail traveller. It released alright with the boom swinging to starboard entirely out of control. I hesitate to put the blame on Baladin just because I had the engine fixed but you never know.

After peace descended and we had got ourselves sorted out we followed the coast pass Zeebrugge and then I misread the buoys. The chart says they are yellow, in reality they are orange but from a distance they looked red. I hadn't seen Sea Breeze for ages but then she had taken a course which put her much further off the coast. Howard told me later how they had had to remove some wire that had become wrapped around the propeller.

Ahead of me I could see the ferry leaving the south side for Flushing so I followed it over, meanwhile I espied Sea Breeze hugging the north bank.

11
Holland

I caught up with Sea Breeze in the lock at Flushing, but being the last in I was therefore last out and being the smallest and slowest I could not keep up with the others with the result that the swing bridge closed on three of us including a catamaran from Faversham.

I decided it would be an opportune moment to top up my main fuel tank so I drew alongside the canal wall to attach a mooring line around a bollard which was on a level with my head. Unfortunately a dog carne along with designs on this bollard which had nothing to do with mooring lines, with the result that he piddled all over my hands just as I was making fast. So much for my baptism in Holland.

I eventually caught up with the other boats having negotiated a couple of cantilever bridges and made for Middleburgh which led off on the port hand side of the canal.

Berths were hard to find but there was a lifting bridge in the middle of town so I was able to go through and find a slot inside.

Middleburgh proved to be a most clean and attractive little town. The yacht club and its facilities were equally good and far superior and cheaper than say Ramsgate.

The following day I planned as a day of rest. Baladin was filthy from the dirt at Dunkerque: it really is an unclean atmosphere with a variety of coloured smoke belching forth night and day from the local industry. I had washing to do, trousers to mend and fresh provisions to acquire but above all this I felt positively scruffy. All these huge yachts came in with their crews dressed immaculately in white flannels and blazers and for comparison I wore an old shirt and gardening trousers. I decided to buy some trousers. Visiting one shop a very attractive assistant came to my aid but she could not speak English. There are times when I despair at the educational standards when foreigners cannot speak our language but this young lady was so kind I could excuse her. She did however offer me a pair which I could see would not fit my ample girth but which information I was incapable of conveying to her except of course by actually trying them on. This I did and the poor girl could not contain her merriment. She then tried the tape measure around my waist and though I found the experience pleasurable, her hands could not meet to pass one end of the tape to the other. Eventually I made my purchase and if nothing else I knew Baladin would approve.

I checked over the boat and found the beer cans in the forward locker were wet. How this came to be I know not but we couldn't have them going rusty so I was forced to drink the lot.

The evening became dark and sultry and the milk I had bought that morning already curdled, later the storm broke with thunder and lightning but somehow it missed us.

Howard and Sue had decided to take off for a week on their own so I set out up the Valcheren Canal with just a genoa and a following wind. It was warm, peaceful and calm, pretty little houses dotted the canal banks and people walking along the towpath would when seeing the red ensign give a wave and a friendly greeting.

After about two and a half miles you enter a lock and then when through that you are disgorged into a vast expanse of water called VEERSE MEER. It embraces numerous islands of all shapes and sizes with mooring and barbecue facilities.

Apart from the cattle and the birds they are uninhabited. There are hundreds of craft of all descriptions, yachts, speed boats, dinghies and surf boards, motor boats and gin palaces and of course the large commercial vessels plying their trade.

I found a small crescent shaped bay on the island of HARINGVRETER where I tied up alongside a pontoon. To go ashore you just slipped off your footwear and waded in about eighteen inches of water. It is hard to believe that this oasis of tranquillity could lie within such a busy waterway. I spent days in bare feet exploring every inch of the island. Ponies roamed freely and there were so many different types of our feathered friends and butterflies it was almost as though it were a sanctuary.

This was such a contrast with the buffeting one gets at sea. Here the land was steady and the wind whistling in the shrouds was replaced by the birds calling in the trees.

Wandering over the fields my mind went back to Robinson Crusoe and wondered whether he felt the peace and quiet of his island as I did on mine. From these fleeting thoughts it was but a short step to Treasure Island which in turn prompted me to bury or conceal my own treasure so if any of you are fortunate enough to visit this island and want your children off your hands for a couple of hours then I suggest you give them a compass and these clues. Let them wade ashore and start looking.

Look for a mooring that looks like an 'H' your right arm facing the pond and the gate.
Steer a course bearing 172
Until a cattle pen hoves into view
Look behind you for the spire at Veere
A bearing of 308 it should be near.
Follow the pathway until you see
A mooring that looks like an inverted 'V'
When the compass reads three score less two
Turn your back it's in front of you
Not buried but lying in bush and in birch
Just ten yards more is the end of your search.

The object is a small plastic bottle containing a message and a coin. It is wrapped in a plastic bag and tied up with spun yarn. If any youngster should find it, I suggest they should replace it with their own message for someone else to find and they can use the same clues.

Time passed all too quickly but eventually I had to leave my island and as I slipped my warps, I gave a nostalgic last look and headed for Kamper land.

There are two marinas here, one costs just over £2 per night and the other is free and close to the village. I chose to stay at the former merely because of its superior facilities, though it did mean a pleasant hike of a mile to the shopping centre. The weather continued glorious and the delightful little houses were a joy to see. Their gardens were a stunning display of colours almost matching my sunburnt nose which had started to peel and bleed.

In preparation for my return trip I spent the following day checking all the gear which was just as well as I found the sheer pin on the outboard grossly misshapen. In the evening I motored over to Veere but finding the harbour terribly crowded I tied up to a pontoon outside. This was quite satisfactory except for an inconsiderate speed boat enthusiast speeding past in the early hours of the morning.

Veere had retained its old historical character and was not marred by modern architecture. I visited the local museum which is mainly given over to photographs of the years of occupation. I still find it hard to believe that this most beautiful land with such happy friendly people could have been ravished in such a treacherous manner.

I briefly saw Sea Breeze but they took off to moor at one of the islands, meanwhile Baladin came in for a lot of attention from some Dutch folk which made her more conceited than she already was.

On the Friday I departed with sadness knowing I was leaving such a haven of peace and beauty, with the sweetness of the air the colours, the friendliness and the unhurried pace of life. Someday I will return, sorry someday we will return.

Back to the canal with its locks and bridges mingling with other vessels bound for unknown destinations. Needless to say my slowness meant that others beat me to the locks so I soon became used to being shut out. If there is one thing sailing teaches you it is patience. I was in no hurry nor was I keen to tie up alongside and tempt another Dutch dog to take liberties with me.

I arrived at Vlissingen (I still prefer the old name of Flushing even if it does suggest it is something to do with the toilet) and tied up in the marina.

Howard and Sue arrived later and the following day we set off with only one lock to negotiate before we reached the open sea.

12
Homeward Bound

Once through the lock it would have been prudent to hoist the sails in the comparative comfort of the harbour. Prudence is not my strong point but in any case being on my own I like plenty of room and with all these yachts and motor boats milling around I did not have that luxury so waited until I got out into the estuary. I had forgotten the current was running at about 2½ knots and it was quite rough, but in no time at all it had swept me down onto a red port hand can buoy. The colour of the buoy was immaterial but the fact it left a red mark on my starboard quarter made it very material. It is a good job these little Corribees are strong boats for I am sure others would have had a hole in the side. It was also fortunate that it didn't hit the outboard for surely I would have lost that but maybe this was one of Baladin's little ploys which did not succeed.

The weather deteriorated somewhat and with the wind over tide it soon became quite rough. I didn't have my wet gear on and was unable to leave the tiller to remedy this omission with the result I was soon soaked to the skin and cold. The seas were cascading over the cabin and some must have found its way into the echo sounder with the result that it ceased to function. I had carefully stowed everything away in the cabin, yet all I could hear was objects crashing from side to side.

There was a temptation to seek refuge in Zeebrugge but as Baladin was just flying along, it would have been callous of me to deprive her of a little bit of exhibitionism. I was not reefed down nor was I wearing a storm jib.

Very soon my charts were wet, and the boat was not steady enough to use my binoculars and my spectacles were so rimed with salt I could neither see through them nor clean them.

I had to rely on memory insofar as buoys and bearings were concerned. But eventually I entered the tranquillity of Blankenberge Yacht Haven. It is true I had to move my berth three times but at last I was able to open the cabin and view the chaos before me.

Sea Breeze had preceded me and Howard sat up until midnight trying to locate the problem with the echo sounder, but without success. On the Sunday I bought a new one, but it wouldn't work either so I surmised that it must be the transducer that was the problem.

Time did not permit me to do anything about the echo sounder so I would have to depart without that vital piece of assurance. This time I wore the top half of my wet gear hoping indeed that fresh rain water would wash out some of the salt in my trousers. It did.

I kept further off shore for obvious reasons but again it was wind over tide so it was bumpy and lumpy, and then I heard noises in the cabin, no not again, crash that must be the radio, crash that must be the kettle, crash that must be the echo sounder. THE ECHO SOUNDER my new bloody echo sounder Hell Hell Hell. My charts are all wet again I really must get a plastic envelope for them, but today is a carbon copy of yesterday only worse, my tobacco and matches are wet. I cannot see to read my charts and now I cannot even have a smoke.

Nieuwpoort was a welcome sight, but the seas were still rough and as I went forward to drop the genoa I took care to tie myself to Baladin. The sail proved a little stubborn but with a bit of coaxing and a few bruises she came down.

Tired wet cold and hungry I tied up and went below. I tidied the cabin, lit the paraffin lamp, battened down the hatches, put on dry clothes then went ashore for a shower, following which I prepared the customary fare on Baladin comprising tinned chopped pork, tinned potatoes and tinned mushy peas.

When the three of us discussed this trip Sue suggested that one night she would cook for all three, and then the next night I would reciprocate. Now Sue is an excellent cook but she's only ever had one meal on Baladin, and when I suggested she and Howard joined me again Sue volunteered to waive the arrangement and invite me on to Sea Breeze. I wonder why.

The marina provided bicycles for visitors so we took advantage of the offer to go into town for petrol and provisions. Then the rain started, it just bucketed down. Just when we were due to leave I had engine problems which Howard managed to fix, then Sea Breeze acquired a rope's end round the screw.

I think Sue looked at these misfortunes as bad omens and appeared quite relieved when we decided to defer our departure until the following day. I had experienced some more water in the cabin so utilised the time to trace the cause. Apparently the port side hatch runner had at some time had an extra hole put in the cabin roof to fix it, but it was never used. It was duly plugged but heavy seas soon find any weaknesses.

This days delay meant we were running behind schedule, so the next day instead of making for Dunkerque we decided to press on to Calais.

We set off at 0815 against wind and tide. At 1220 the tide turned and the wind veered around from the south to the north west. This favourable turn prompted me to take advantage by topping up the main petrol tank, but when I tried the engine she wouldn't work. There are times when I truly believe Baladin does this on purpose, but there was no time for reprovals because she just took off. Although it was blowing a force 5 conditions were excellent and we were making just over 4 knots.

Approaching Calais I tried the engine again but without success, so I dropped the main in order to sail in under the genoa. Now we all know how busy Calais is, and the entrance is comparatively narrow considering the traffic that uses it. We also no doubt appreciate that when a ferry or other large vessels are entering or leaving everything else stops, well we arrived and with numerous other small boats meandered around awaiting the signal that would permit us to enter. Of course all the other boats were under power, they had dropped their sails and they had no objection to the presence of an engine hanging over their stern. Why cannot Baladin reconcile herself to this evil necessity, but I digress, the signal went up and we all converged on the entrance and what did Baladin do? She has a petulant mood and takes her time. The other boats have all entered but as we arrived the signal tells us to keep out. There was no way I could comply. A noise from astern heralded the arrival of another ferry so what the hell do we do. If I go to port I'll be trapped because that is where she will berth, if I go to starboard she'll take my wind and her wash will put me on the rocks. I decided to stay in the middle and pray. Baladin was completely unruffled by all this. I could imagine her saying, "Don't worry I've tackled bigger ships than that." If she was thinking of Charlie at least we hit him, but this monster was really right up our stern. Normally the harbour master would have got on the tannoy and told us to "get the hell out of it", but he didn't which I can only attribute to his understanding the problem or failing that he must have been intimidated by Baladin.

Well we survived and in fact were only twenty minutes behind Sea Breeze, though Sue did express the view that I should rename Baladin "Bad Penny" because she always turns up.

A Yamaha dealer picked the engine and myself up from the marina after my amateurish efforts had failed to resolve the problem. It was now Friday and I wanted to be in Ramsgate today but it was not to be, anyway, Mr Yamaha stripped the engine down and did a wonderful job. I cannot praise him enough not only for his ability but the fact he gave me immediate attention. I was of course embarrassed when I found I did not have sufficient funds to pay him but that is another story.

Howard and Sue were going to leave today but bad weather kept them in harbour. I must confess that I took selfish comfort at this because the wretched engine had really made me feel low in spirits.

Saturday dawned with a beautiful sky and a good forecast so I decided not to use the engine but sail all the way irrespective of my speed. I soon lost sight of Sea Breeze but I would see them at Ramsgate. I lay back with a can of beer and a pipe full of tobacco. It was nice to be going home but it was also nice to reflect on this last three weeks and to enjoy the current sail. I was completely oblivious to the fact that I had made an error in my decision to sail without using the engine and the longer I did this then so the problem would magnify. I did not come to my senses until I saw on the horizon this brown streak. I have in the past often seen this and have treated it as a heat haze, however some time later I noticed white crests, which again was surprising because they were not to be seen elsewhere and then it slowly dawned on me. My navigation is as I have said earlier based on a speed of 4 knots and on a straight run I change course every hour. What I had been doing was changing course on the hour when I had only been doing three knots and what I could see in front of me was the sea breaking over the Goodwins Knoll. I promptly started the engine and escaped from that situation a wiser man. It took me nine hours to get to Ramsgate which was longer than it should have been but then as I said I was enjoying the sail.

Ramsgate was crowded but it did not matter as I would leave early on Sunday morning. I checked everything and found my navigation lights wouldn't work. Whether it was the battery or a fuse I knew not but I keep a spare paraffin lamp for emergencies like this, and tied it to the pulpit. The light flickered its red and green rays, and it made me realise how much we miss these old lamps and the warm homely light they give but enough of that. At 0500 I departed for the last leg.

The wind was almost non-existent and while the trip should take 10 hours I only had fuel for 8, I therefore decided to motor sail for 6 hours in order to take fullest advantage of the tidal stream and hope for a wind improvement. On reaching the Whitaker Beacon I cut the engine, dropped the genoa and hoisted the wind chute aided by a spinnaker pole. I had the chute out the port side and main to starboard. Progress was minimal, no wind, the sea was like a mirror with barely a ripple to mar its surface. One could not imagine a more beautiful day, nor indeed could one imagine a day at sea that is so free of danger. In conditions like this it is easy to get complacent; it is easy to do things without thinking them through. I sat in the cockpit pondering my next move and how I could get just a little movement out of Baladin because we were now becalmed and then I looked at the spinnaker pole, of course it is too heavy for these conditions. I went up the port side to remove it and before I knew what had happened my weight had caused the boom to swing right over to port. It caught me right across the chest, I fell with both feet under the lower guard rail and in the water. One is always learning a lesson the hard way but really when one comes to analyse it, it was thoughtless, careless and patently obvious after the event as to what can and did happen.

I eventually tied up in the marina at 1630 having taken nearly 12 hours which is a long time to be sitting at the tiller. I really must consider an auto-helm. I had exactly half a pint of petrol left, I was battered bruised and brown. I was scarred, tired, hungry and dirty but it was all a wonderful experience. Baladin was of course exemplary - the trouble is she knows it.

13
Take Care of Him

I planned a trip to Brightlingsea but the weather in the week preceding my departure had been atrocious. I had invited Howard to join me and had arranged to pick him up from the jetty at Burnham on the Friday morning. The sky was black with fast moving clouds in angry turmoil disgorging their contents on the unfortunates below. The shipping forecast was for winds force 6-7 and they were absolutely correct. I pondered on the wisdom of going to sea in these conditions but I had absolute faith in Baladin's ability and had also made thorough preparations.

Sue drove Howard to the jetty and as we waved goodbye she said, "Take care of him Geoff." Somehow those words had a profound effect on me as I realised that I had suddenly in the most inclement conditions acquired a responsibility not normally experienced in my customary single handed sailing.

At 13.20 we hoisted the storm jib and put a reef in the main. The strong S.W. wind took us downstream against the tide. I had chosen this particular time in order to take the short cut over the Ray Sands. High tide was 15.19 by which time I hoped to be clear of them, but in any case with such heavy seas we needed plenty of water beneath us. Surprisingly it was an exceedingly good sail even if we did have our gunwales under the water for most of the time with an occasional deluge into the cockpit. We arrived in the mouth of the Colne at 16.00 and at 17.00 I decided to drop the canvas. I did not say anything to Howard but Sue's words were with me, to the extent I wouldn't let him leave the cockpit so I went forward to drop the jib. I had started the engine and Howard took the tiller. Then after tying myself to the boat I crawled forward on hands and knees. From where I was I could not hear the engine and the forecastle was so lively I was forced to lie on my stomach. There is not a lot of room on the Corribee forecastle and with my liberal proportions there was even less. Hanging on for dear life with one hand I tried to pull the sail down. Whilst doing this the bows would rise violently then when it reached its peak it would drop leaving me in mid-air until she dug her nose into a trough when the deck and my body made impact and the cleat under my stomach just knocked the wind out of me. The wet sails were then slapped around my face and this became even more violent when the jib sheet shackle came adrift. I eventually got things under control and secure.

It was a relief to get back to the cockpit even though I was bruised and physically exhausted. I really must conceive some idea to do all this from the cockpit but I was indeed relieved to have Howard aboard.

Sue had motored to Brightlingsea to meet us and the relief on her face was a sight to behold.

I made the return journey alone but although the S.W. wind was on the nose going over the sands we made (with engine complimenting the sails) good progress.

Few boats had been out this weekend which became obvious as we went through the moorings at Burnham. Baladin looked as though she had had a rough time but she still manages to reflect a proud and cocky appearance that boasted of another achievement.

14
Visitors

Over the years a number of friends have sailed with me aboard Baladin and the following accounts reflect but a few. First we have Mr. Ed, a business colleague and great friend from New York. Now Mr. Ed served with distinction in the U.S. Navy in the Pacific War area. From this I assumed that Mr. Ed would be nautically aware of sailing ships and all that is associated with them. I had always been told "Never assume anything", but I obviously don't take advice easily.

I gave Mr. Ed the times of the trains and where to board it and where to disembark. I assumed he would adhere to it but he didn't. He left from a different station at a different time and alighted at one where I was not due to meet him. No harm was done and we met and drove to the marina. I noticed he was wearing hard soled shoes and assumed he would be carrying deck shoes in his bag. He didn't. He was in need of some cigarettes and I assumed the shop at the marina sold them. They didn't. My earlier assumption that he knew something about sailing was also faulted.

In spite of this we had a wonderful day's sailing including dropping the hook in a little bay where we had lunch. Weighing the anchor proved a little difficult but after much cussing and swearing she was straight up and down. Little did I know that Mr. Ed had taped this charade.

Eventually the time came to go back to the marina, but getting into the marina with its cross currents can be very tricky so I normally lash the tiller fore and aft and steer solely by the outboard. I asked Mr. Ed to lash the tiller as I assumed being an ex-navy man he would know about these things.

At a crucial moment I found Baladin was not responding, she was sluggish and slow to answer. I had to do a complete turn and try again with the same result. I threw her into reverse to avoid the other boats and then I saw the tiller swinging free and thwarting every movement of the engine so another assumption backfired on me but for all that it was great to have him aboard.

Then there was Irv. Now Irv has a very nice sailing boat in Seattle. In fact although we didn't go sailing in it he did take me aboard so it was only natural that he should join me on one of his visits. We had not pre-arranged this but Irv arrived with all the necessary sailing gear.

It was a beautiful day but only a little wind. We tacked back and forth across the river without making any headway. Now those river banks have little identifying features by which you can judge your progress except one. There is a board that forbids landing or anchoring, just one board. Irv suddenly tumbled to the fact that we did not appear to be getting anywhere.

"Geoff," he said, "that board was there an hour ago."

"No Irv the banks have numerous such signs." I do not think he was convinced.

Then we have Dick. He hails from Chicago and had a beautiful 27 ft yacht. We went sailing one evening on Lake Michigan and I just relaxed and enjoyed myself being unaware that his crew, namely Dave Walton and John were like their skipper unfamiliar with the ways of the sea but that's by the way. Dick and his wife Lil came down to Baladin. Now Lil is not exactly enamoured with the water so we went for a gentle motor downstream.

I trust my other guests will forgive me but I am sure they will understand when I say that the following visitors gave me extreme pleasure.

One Friday afternoon I said to my office colleagues, "If anyone would like to join me for a sail on Sunday morning you would be most welcome."

There was a deathly silence, all heads were glued to the files in front of them, no one looked up. One could almost hear their thoughts, "Are you kidding, this guy's a sailing disaster."

I was about to enter my office when young Sally spoke up. "Does that include me?" The question momentarily threw me.

I hadn't expected any of the girls would want to sail, especially one as attractive as Sally.

"Why yes, yes of course it does," I replied, "but there are two conditions. Number one you do not tell my wife and number two you bring a chaperone."

Sunday morning broke with a strong breeze and spasmodic sights of the sun. I prepared Baladin for my guests and waited. I was standing on the pontoon when from afar I saw three most beautiful young ladies adorned in hot pants and tight fitting sleeveless blouses. As they came nearer it was obvious that any one of them could have graced the cover of a beauty magazine. The other boat owners just froze, their eyes riveted on this apparition of feminine beauty. Their amazement was only exceeded when they saw them being assisted aboard Baladin by this old codger. Thoughts of old fiddles and sweet tunes flitted through my mind but I was careful to avert my eyes from any of my friends in the marina. No way was I going to allow them to muscle in on the act.

We passed between the lines of boats with this bevy of beauties gracing the deck. I hoisted the sails and away we went. Unfortunately it was choppier than I thought with the result that the girls from the waist up soon became soaking wet from the spindrift. We had been out for some time and I thought we would return to the marina where the girls were going to prepare a light lunch. I asked Sally to take the tiller and showed her a point on land that she should aim for while I went up forward. Now Sally drives a car, she is used to swinging the wheel to the left when she wants to go left, she did the same with the tiller with the result that Baladin nearly keeled over - I was kneeling on the foredeck clinging to the mast for dear life with the water half way up my thighs. The girls were yelling and I could see the sea pouring into the cockpit. Now they were really wet, soaked from head to toe and cold with lt.

I didn't say anything to the girls but it was Baladin up to her tricks, she was jealous and while she can show off she objects when I do. Order was soon restored but I suggested the girls went below to dry off. Two of them did so, but Sally braved it out up top, however it was not long before two very pale young ladies with a slight shade of green emerged clutching the bucket. I gave one a reefer jacket and the other a blanket to keep them warm, but then of course we had to run the gauntlet of the other boats and my young ladies did not have quite the same appearance or composure and elegance as when they left. Their make-up was running, their hair was all over the place and their blouses were sticking to them; they really did look bedraggled and I was the cause of it.

Once we had tied up and got the stove working the girls dried out and prepared a meal.

It goes without saying that others had followed with interest the events on Baladin and like a honey pot we soon became the target of much attention.

"Is there anybody aboard?" It was Terry; I recognised the voice. Is there anybody aboard? He knew damn fine who was on board. He clambered aboard with a pack of beer. "Oh sorry Geoff I didn't know you had visitors." Like hell he didn't and he said it without blushing.

"Where's Richard?" I enquired after introducing him to my female crew.

"He's not well, he's gone home." Well he must have had a miracle cure because before Terry had completed the sentence Richard was also aboard.

All too soon the time came to say goodbye. I hope they will come again. It does an old man's heart a lot of good even if his blood pressure does rise, but don't tell my wife.

15
Two Men in a Boat – by "Baladin"

For some time I had had a premonition that the Master was up to something, and when I saw him spreading out some charts I knew he was planning another cross channel trip. The biggest surprise however was the fact that he was not going alone. Evidently Mike was going to join us. Now I know nothing about Mike, but as he had agreed to come I imagine he must possess first class references that would qualify him as idiot of the year.

One thing I did learn is that although Mike is somewhat younger (but then who isn't) they are both Sagittarians and indeed share the same birthday. This knowledge came about when I heard Mike saying that Sagittarians were extroverts, outspoken and forceful, further they speak their minds and do not take offence.

I was going to say you didn't need to be an idiot to know that Mike was priming the Master for two weeks of verbal abuse, but of course the Master didn't see it, but then Mike forgot to mention that Sagittarians don't listen either.

Sunday was to be the day of departure and so with a S.W. force 5 wind forecast we set off on the ebb tide thereby making good progress. We changed course at the Whitaker Beacon and beaded for the Edinburgh Channel. We passed the Tongue Light Ship with that haunting noise that you hear long before you see the ship. Going past the East Margate buoy and the North Foreland we eventually arrived in Ramsgate in just over ten hours.

All was peaceful aboard though now and again I did hear the Master yelling, "You're off course, get closer to the wind, watch your compass." Low rumbled responses came from the deck hand which sounded something like "Bligh". The Master who gets a little conceited about his navigational abilities didn't want some slap happy land lubber nullifying all his fine work.

The following morning the Master was up before 0500 and suddenly decided we would go to Dover. Mike was still asleep, and didn't wake up until we had cleared Ramsgate harbour. With bleary eyes and tousled hair he poked his head out of the cabin. What he must have thought I have no idea, but if he had had the sense to speak to me first I could have told him to expect the unexpected, as it turned out he suddenly found himself on the high seas with no shower, no shave and no breakfast. It was as though the days of the press gang had returned.

It was a good sail taking us only three hours to reach Dover where we dropped anchor in the bay pending instructions from the harbour control as to when we should enter the Wellington Basin.

Dover is as is to be expected a very busy ferry terminal, but the noise from the hovercraft drowns all conversation and the smell from the constant odour of petrol and diesel fumes forever invades the nostrils.

In view of the early start they both decided to get their heads down and catch up on some sleep, but before they could do so they were hailed from the seawall by an elderly lean looking man. He introduced himself as Tommy and wanted to know what the conditions were like in the basin and where were we going. Tommy came aboard and told us that his wooden motor sailer was anchored in Pegwell Bay, and he had caught the bus into Dover to check the conditions and facilities. We gathered that Tommy was also going to Calais and he said he might see us outside the following day.

Tuesday morning broke with a pretty good forecast for the crossing. The winds were 3 to 4 from the N.W. Visibility was about two miles. At 11.20 they opened the dock gates and all these small vessels crowded together like a flock of sheep until they were disgorged into the canal outside but then the harbour patrol kept us all back until the hovercraft had cleared the entrance. Unfortunately we were delayed for over 50 minutes.

Eventually we cleared the harbour entrance, but the thought did cross my mind that in view of the speed of these hovercraft one can understand the authorities taking precautions which somehow highlighted our arrival yesterday where the Master made his entrance in a very cavalier fashion.

We passed the South Goodwin Lightship at 12.54 and were in the first shipping lane by 13.20. The Master has already told you of his habit of navigating on the basis of my doing 4 knots so as he is too mean to buy a log I sometimes fool him by going faster than he thinks me capable. This passage presented the right opportunity with the result he misjudged the tidal stream and our first sight of land was Dunkerque West.

"What's that?" said the crew.

"Oh," said the Master with an air of authority. "That is Dunkerque." The only way he knew it was Dunkerque, was because the sky is always so full of smoke of every imaginable colour.

"What are we doing off Dunkerque?" asked the crew.

In an airy manner the Master said off handedly, "By coming this way we pick up the current in the Dunkerque Roads, it takes us right into Calais." Whether Mike was fooled or not I don't know, but I do know this: the charts did not reflect any course which showed us coming down the Dunkerque Roads.

We sailed into Calais at 18.00 but we had to wait until high tide before we could get a berth in the yacht basin, so we tied up alongside a Dutch boat called "Bolleket". Her crew was made up of mother and father and two sons, one of whom had his girlfriend Janet aboard. Peter and Janet spoke very good English and it was not long before conversation got around to the forthcoming wedding of Prince Andrew and Sarah Ferguson. They were so interested that Mike gave them the English newspapers we had on board; and then to our surprise the mother cooked some fresh mackerel and passed them over. I know the Master was feeling a bit peckish and the galley slave was making no move to produce a meal so this gift was indeed manna.

It was 01.30 before we reached the tranquil waters of the marina. We left Bolleket outside as she was going up the coast but bad weather had forced her back and the following day she too entered the marina with Tommy from Dover who had just arrived on his motor sailer 'Eander'.

The Master had intended going South to Boulogne until he realised that we could only get out of the basin at high tide and as the tide ebbs north, we would be fighting it all the way unless of course we chose to swing round a buoy for six hours, so a change of plan was made and we would go north. Unfortunately the weather deteriorated with winds ranging from force 6 to 8 so we stayed in harbour.

Tommy joined Mike and the Master in a rail trip to Boulogne to review the marina there and they were amazed at the congested state of the mooring facilities. Really this should not have been surprising considering the weather and also the fact that Boulogne is a better starting off port for going south than Calais.

While they were away a 27 ft Westerly from Leigh on Sea tied up alongside us with John and his wife aboard. The Master would however constantly refer to their vessel's name as 'IN IT UP IT'' as he found it easier to remember than the other way round namely 'TIPUTINI'. I mention this merely to illustrate a possible reason for our misadventures. If he cannot remember a name how on earth can he plot a course but then of course we know about that.

Mike proved to be an exceedingly good cook and his culinary attributes were improving with every day. The finesse with which he opened cans was a sight to behold, and the artistry employed in frying broken eggs could only be appreciated by someone suffering from pangs of hunger.

A charming Dutch couple Henri and Allie arrived in their yacht 'Squall' and the following evening Tommy invited them and the Master and Mate aboard for a wine and cheese supper. It really was a most civilised affair and so different from that to which they are accustomed to receive aboard me. The Mate, seeking to broaden his mind was asking Allie to translate certain English words. She obligingly complied with his request until the word "flasher" was put forward.

Mike did not quite follow the answer so asked her to clarify it by putting it back into English. The answer became "pencil vendor". This highly amused the listeners, but I am still not sure whether Master and Mate were quietly having their legs pulled.

Whilst they were on Tommy's boat Peter and Janet had stepped aboard me and left some gifts, namely a pipe for the Master and cigarette rolling equipment for the Mate. It was a very kind and touching gesture which brought forth such eloquent words of appreciation the like of which I thought they were incapable, especially as I had witnessed a constant barrage of rudeness and coarseness, vulgarity and blasphemy since the moment we left the Crouch, but having said that they really do get on together and the interchange of harsh words is merely a veneer which marks a great companionship.

The high winds kept up for four days which merely succeeded in keeping all the boats in the marina for a longer period than they had intended, but even high winds do not go on forever, so at 06.30 on Sunday morning they locked out and with a S.SW wind and the current with us we made good progress.

We passed Gravelines at 08.35, Dunkerque West at 09.45, Dunkerque East at 11.10. We reached the TRAE PEGER at 14.35 and sailed into Nieuwport in Belgium at 16.30. During the trip I could sense that the Master was simmering for the deck hand was rubbing him up the wrong way. It wasn't the constant reference to "Bligh". It wasn't the lateness of the meals. He didn't even say anything when the cutlery was thrown overboard, no the problem was the unseaman-like manner of his crew. Now who would call a fender a bumper but a landlubber (or maybe someone trying to rub the skipper up the wrong way) who would wind a rope round his elbow like an old washerwoman but a landlubber.

The Master would cringe at the sight and sound of such activities. Next we would be subject to a musical interlude. The galley slave should have been below preparing sandwiches, instead he was having a quiet smoke and tuning the radio to some modern pop music. To drown this monstrous noise the Master would start to sing (I use the term advisedly) then from below the volume would be increased, then from above the raucous bellow of a bull purported to drown all noises.

Henri and Allie aboard Squall arrived and we caught a fleeting glance of Bolleket when she came into refuel.

Gale force winds confined us to harbour but on Tuesday we decided to depart. The forecast was S.W. force 4 to 5 gusting 6 so they put up the storm jib and one reef in the main. We cast off at 14.30 cleared the harbour entrance at 14.55 and then all hell let loose.

The combined efforts of sails and engine proved ineffective, then we were picked up like a babe in arms and thrown to one side. The wind was now 6 to 7 in strength so Master decided to abort the trip. The crew was quiet so I can only imagine he was in agreement. On returning to the marina they walked out to the end of the pier. The sand being whipped off the beach stung every exposed part of the body as though one was being massaged with sandpaper.

Then the Master quoted to his crew the words of an unknown old seafarer as though they were of his own origin.

"I would rather be in here wishing I was out there, than out there wishing I was in here." If he was looking for some recognition of this profound piece of stolen wisdom he didn't get it.

The crew did a good job as refuelling engineer and he was also excellent at provisioning ship.

They took a day off to travel by tram to Ostend but time was getting short and the return journey home could not be delayed so on Wednesday at 12.30 we cast off and with a N.NW wind looked for a leisurely sail down to Dunkerque. Well it was certainly leisurely but with winds no more than 1 to 2 the current carried us towards Ostend. We got to the West Stroomback buoy at 13.05 and Middle Kerk at 15.45. It hurts me to say this but there was only one thing to do and that was to motor sail and start that infernal engine; this they did at

16.00. Under such relaxing conditions the Master and crew became apathetic to the extent they didn't top up the main fuel tank so at 17.05 when they took the sails down the engine cut out. Normally this would not have been a problem except that an old coastal freighter was bearing down on us. They could of course have hoisted the sails but as there was no wind it would not have helped so while Mike was feverishly transferring the petrol the Master was doing a bit of praying allied to expressing doubts about the parentage of the skipper of the oncoming freighter. Somehow we knew this huge black monster had seen us but was intent on giving us a fright. Maybe they had read the Master's mind. Anyway they missed us by 20 yards or more and the resulting wash did not make the task of transferring the fuel any easier.

We finally tied up in Dunkerque at 19.50. The Master and crew went along to the yacht club where they indulged themselves in a fine meal. This was most appreciated by the Master as the previous evening the Galley boy had produced hard boiled eggs and as a substitute he opened a tin of corned beef, minced it up with powdered potatoes and fried the result with mushy peas. The Master appears to me most hypocritical when he cannot cook himself but expects everyone else to do better. Of course he may have a point when Mike followed the main course with mouldy bread and tea with curdled milk.

As a result of their over indulgence they slept late and missed the shipping forecast. There had been gale force winds in the night but they had died down and while the sky presented a blanket of ugly clouds the Master decided we would make the cross channel trip to Ramsgate. At 06.45 we cast off and as we proceeded along the channel to the harbour entrance we noticed the fishing vessels coming in. Their crews were poking fingers into the air which we thought was rather vulgar. We did not realise until later that they were trying to convey to us the strength of the wind. In fact we were picked up, thrown 180 degrees and with water pouring into the cockpit the Master decided to abort the voyage. In view of the fact that we were still in the harbour this was no doubt a prudent decision. It was at this stage the Master noticed that the storm cones had been raised though it was noticeable by his silence that he did not tell Mike.

That afternoon they walked to the lighthouse and watched two other yachts battling against the elements. The one going south returned to harbour, but the other going north with an ebb tide and a force 7 S.W. wind was almost jet propelled. That evening the BBC gave gale warnings force 8/9 but at 15.00 they gave a forecast for the next 24 hours which sounded a little more promising being S.W. 5 to 7 reducing to 4 later.

Dawn broke on Friday morning but our two sleepy-headed crew didn't see it neither did they hear the weather forecast but the Master tried to convey the impression that he could read the metrological signs and said, "It's going to be a good crossing."

Mike looked sceptical, he had listened to this form of misplaced optimism before. The sun shone brightly as at 07.50 we cast off with a strong westerly breeze. Once clear of the harbour we set a course of 322 degrees. At 10.45 we reached Ruytingen and changed to 315 degrees. By 11.00 the wind had freshened to force 3 but the sun continued to beat down on us. By 11.35 we reached Sandettie and altered course again. At 18.10 we were off the North Goodwin Lightship and we reached Ramsgate at 19.30 tying up at 19.45 in the outer harbour.

The crossing was comfortable and enjoyable though with the light winds it took us that much longer. We had been surprised at the lack of other yachts in the channel but we soon found out why. The outer harbour at Ramsgate was crowded but when they saw us coming in flying the yellow flag they gathered around to find out where we had come from and what the crossing was like.

Apparently the forecast the Master missed was a prediction of gale force winds. It did his ego untold good to have made a passage that the larger boats would not attempt. In reality the forecast was 24 hours too early because on the Saturday no one moved with winds of force 6/7/8 thereby allowing the crew to experience the culinary arts of the fish and chip shop.

Sunday arrived bathed in glorious sunshine, there was not a ripple on the water and a slight breeze was barely discernible.

At 07.55 we set off and as we cleared the harbour entrance I heard the Master say, "We are in for trouble, we're going to motor sail the whole way." I must confess I thought it a bit odd when there wasn't a cloud in the sky, and if he really believed what he was saying why did he not put up a storm jib or prepare the main for reefing? We passed North Foreland at 08.50 and the Longnose buoy at 09.15. The wind freshened a little from the N.E. but the sea was still like a mill pond, even the merchant ships moored off Margate looked as though they were sitting on a sea of cotton wool.

Three porpoises passed a mile away on our port side and the buildings on the north Kent coast were clear and defined. All was quiet on board, there was very little conversation which may have been due to it being the end of their holiday, but I rather suspect the Master was still sure the weather would deteriorate.

At 10.00 they took a bearing from the Tongue Sands and the Lightship. At 10.30 we entered the Edinburgh Channel and at the same time we saw dark clouds gathering on the horizon. The Master asked Mike to top up the petrol tank, check that all below was secure and put on his wet gear. Before all this had been accomplished the heavens opened up. There was thunder and lightning with torrential rain, visibility dropped to half a mile. The Master only had time to put on the top half of his waterproofs. We did not reef down as it was too dangerous to go forward and change the jib. At 11.20 we reached Black Deep 11. It was here the Master decided to depart from the charted course. He was going over the Foulness Sands on a falling tide. There was absolutely no conversation on board, the Master with left hand on the tiller kept a constant watch on the compass bearing, the echo sounder and wind indicator. We crept along the edge of the Maplin Sands grabbing a foot here and a foot there. We all dreaded the thought of going aground in this weather and being pounded on the sands but allowances were made for the troughs and peaks.

Through the gloom we could see a North Cardinal buoy. If it was the Sunken Buxey we would be safely over, and would have saved ourselves maybe an hour and a half. It was. A gale was blowing and the seas were just a raging turmoil. We were in the Whittaker Channel at 13.30. The engine was turned off to conserve fuel neither of them wishing to top up in these conditions. A gaff rigged barge tacked across our bows but we had the wind with us, if not the tide which contributed to the lumpy sea conditions.

Mike broke the silence (in fact I didn't know he could keep quiet for so long). Mike said, "I think I can see land on the starboard bow."

Whether it was this sudden expression of nautical terminology which took the Master by surprise or whether he momentarily lost concentration I will never know, all I was aware of was suddenly keeling over at a precarious angle, the Master being jammed upside down in the cockpit well with Mike on top and both of them being soaked with the seas coming inboard. Suddenly from beneath this miniature rugby scrum I heard the words, "Where's the tiller Mike?"

Slowly the storm abated and the rain eased off, the seas calmed down and the white crests were no longer to be seen. Mike managed to get half a gallon of fuel in the tank which could satisfy our immediate needs.

We eventually tied up in Wallasea Marina at 16.00 which brought the holiday to its conclusion.

***

I have purposely held my peace while Baladin wrote the above but although she is held by me in high esteem and indeed affection I must say she is proud, arrogant and bossy. The reader will have observed through these pages how she gets her own back on me, in fact there are times when she is downright embarrassing but I do not believe that just because she is attractive with delightful lines it is any excuse for her outrageous behaviour. The point I am trying to make is that she would have you believe Mike and I were constantly at each other's throats well I can tell you that I have known Mike for over 35 years and the day we start being courteous to one another is the day we fall out, so don't take too much notice of Baladin because she has jealous tendencies too, which is why she and my wife have never met (I shudder to think of the outcome). Anyway Mike and I had a wonderful time and I hope the opportunity arises again whereby we may visit ports south of Calais.

IN SICKNESS AND IN HEALTH   1987

Geoff Shelton

Fear, doubts, apprehensions can all play tricks upon the mind and so it was with me. In mid-December 1988 I took Baladin out of the water and put her on the hard where she was going to undergo a complete overhaul. In a previous magazine it recommended reading 'The Care andRepair of Yachts' by Tony Staton-Bevan. I duly purchased the book and started to explore the secrets of fibreglass boats – it became my evening reading on the train whilst travelling to and from the City.

The more I read the more depressed I became, and the cause – osmosis. I went back to the Autumn '86 magazine and re-read Roy Allgood's account of his experience. I went down to Baladin with the book in one hand and slowly caressed every inch of hull. I was fast becoming neurotic. My beautiful Baladin, my beloved Baladin – how could she be stricken like this? My panic took me to Ernie, the Yacht Broker. "Where can I get a Surveyor?" I pleaded, and poured out my fears. Ernie has a bedside manner, and setting me outside, showed me a boat suffering from osmosis.

"Is it like that?" I didn't think so, and he promised to have a look at Baladin for me. Meanwhile, my friends on the moorings all reassured me that she was fit and healthy.

Alas, the shock of this experience had undermined my own resistance and I too was stricken. I went to my GP. "Is it osmosis, Doctor?" He didn't appear to understand.

"Secondary infection," he snapped, "a virus. Have a week in bed."

Of course my wife now took charge; no matter at what time, day or night, she attended to my every wish. However, as each day saw an improvement, it was not long before my nurse was suggesting I go through the clutter of nautical magazines which were stacked in piles around the bedroom. They went back about eight years, and it was a demand I had been expecting for some time! I started to go through them one by one, and an article here and there I removed.

"Why are you saving these?"

"I thought they might come in useful."

"But they're all about sailing in the Greek Islands."

"So?"

"Well, you are not going there are you?"

I was not sure whether this last was a statement or an inquiry. "A man can dream," I said. "I rather think I'll give these magazines to old George," I went on nobly.

"A good idea," approved my nurse, "he'll enjoy them."

George is a slow reader and very forgetful. In six months' time, he'll offer me all these boating magazines!

'HEY TIMBER!!'
G. W. SHELTON 1987

A friend had invited me to crew for him one Sunday morning in the local Yacht Club race.

We were sitting on his boat enjoying the warmth of the morning sun, when a timber ship passed up stream. This in itself was not an uncommon sight, as there is a wharf about two hundred yards to the west of the marina. She turned round with her bows facing the incoming tide when suddenly she started emitting constant bleeps on her siren.

"I've never heard a navigation signal like that," said someone.

As we looked up it appeared as though she was coming into the marina.

"She bloody well is," yelled someone else and though we were moored away from the action a mad rush ensued towards the incoming vessel. Soon we witnessed masts crashing to the decks as she hit first one boat then another and another at the same time ripping the fingers from the pontoon. Into the middle of all this she dropped her anchor.

The warning signal had allowed the boat owners to vacate their vessels – in fact one young lad was still carrying his breakfast plate.

Boats were drifting upstream still lashed to their fingers and welded together with the mast and rigging of the boat alongside them. Everybody helped with advice, orders instructions, all of which ran contrary to the next man, and none of it was heeded. No one had a knife, no one had any rope. Very soon the police arrived then the fire brigade and the ambulance and the Salvage Corp and the lifeboatmen, though not necessarily in that order. The police took charge in a very quiet and efficient, manner with the fire brigade in assistance.

Fortunately there was no loss of life and no injuries, but dare I say I thought I saw the trace of a smile flickering across the face of the Yacht Broker and the ship repair owner.

AN ABORTED TRIP 1987

The sun was shining as I awoke one Sunday morning in May aboard 'Baladin'.

I was eager to prepare ship for a sail down the river. Whilst engaged in this labour some friends came down the pontoon and said there were five baby ducklings frantically looking for their mother. Without parental care they would not last very long. Someone brought a landing net, I provided a washing up bowl and soon all five ducklings had been captured.

The lady and her son said, "We are just going for a sail. If they are still alive on our return we'll take them to a friend who can take care of them."

I could see my own sail would have to be deferred. Very soon the children came along and started poking through the landing net which covered the basin to stop the ducks escaping. I realised that this frightening experience would probably bring about their early demise whereupon I turned off the drainage cocks in the cockpit of Baladin, filled it with water to the height of the duckboards and brought the ducklings aboard.

Of course the children had to come too, but at least I could keep an eye on them and explained how frightened they would be if a monster was poking them. They soon grasped the lesson and quickly conveyed it to the four year old. When they arrived on board the ducklings did not know how to eat so obviously they were only a few days old. I crumpled up some cornflakes and scattered bran in the water. Very soon they understood what was required of them, however one little fellow was shivering with cold so he was wrapped up and put in the cabin for warmth.

Some three hours later my friends returned and were surprised that the ducklings were still alive, but soon they took them away to a sanctuary where I hoped they would recover and lead a full life.

I never did get that sail, but somehow I had no regrets.

16
High Hopes

I had for some time been thinking of sailing down to the Isle of Wight but had constantly deferred it for the most flimsiest of reasons and that is Baladin has a fin keel, and all the ports between Dover and Newhaven dry out. It's alright for bilge keelers they can sit comfortably on the mud but we do not have that luxury. This appeared to me a very poor excuse, so the decision was taken to go even if it did mean taking about 25 hours from Ramsgate to Newhaven just to avoid dry harbours, anyway at 05.50 on the Saturday morning we set off. We had a moderate S.W. wind and an ebb tide so conditions were perfect.

I had in fact asked Mike to join me but he was graciously otherwise engaged so we went alone. It was very overcast and cloudy and with such a light wind I decided to scrap my charted course through the Edinburgh Channel and see if there was more wind further out going across Sunk Sand and through Fisherman's Gat.

Whether this was wise or not I will never know. Certainly the wind increased, it being now 4 to 5 but visibility was down to less than two miles; in fact I heard on the radio that two ships twenty miles off Ramsgate had collided. I could hear helicopters overhead but could not see any other activity, nevertheless the thought did cross my mind that if the professionals with all the latest navigational aids can do this, what chance do we amateurs have with a compass and echo sounder and a pair of eyes.

We were off N.E. Hook Middle at 08.50 and went through Fisherman's Gat at 11.10. The Tongue Light Ship could be heard long before we could see it, and while I recognise its value to the seafarer its sound is so haunting that all you want to do is to leave it far behind you. I took a bearing of 210 degrees as I lined up the Lightship and the Tongue Sands. I was of course taking the more seaward route. By the time we reached the Longnose at 14.40 the wind was now 5 gusting 6 from the south added to which the tide was against us.

We were in a lumpy sea and just crawling along so at 15.35 the sails were dropped and we relied on the engine. I may have been a little premature in putting this little evolution into practice but other yachtsmen appeared to have the same idea though no doubt their engines were stronger than mine. We eventually arrived in Ramsgate at 17.00.

Obviously Baladin takes priority over one's personal needs so once I had tidied up I went for fuel. There is a fuel tender in the harbour but they do not sell two stroke so one has to climb Jacobs ladder a mere 90 steps plus walking nearly a mile to make the purchase from a local garage. For a port which is a popular jumping off and arrival point for the continent the facilities are abysmal, but after eleven hours at the tiller the exercise no doubt did me some good.

A fitful sleep was disturbed by other yachts leaving at 03.00 at the height of the tide.

My intention the next day was to sail all day long and through the night to Newhaven. With this in mind I cast off at 07.25 and set a course of 190 degrees down the Gulf Stream. The weather was still overcast and cloudy with visibility down to less than two miles. The wind was supposed to veer from S.W. to N.W. but it didn't. It was supposed to rain. It did. It was supposed to be foggy. It was. With winds so light and almost on the nose we motor sailed. In the murky gloom I could see the flashing light of the South Goodwin light ship and the passing ferries were just grey smudges in the distance. In conditions like this one doesn't get too close to Dover harbour and you keep the engine on for greater manoeuvrability. You can see the ferry boat funnels over the sea wall and can therefore tell if one is due to come out but the hovercraft are a different matter. You can hear them miles away but when they start moving they really move, so good eyesight and good anticipation is needed when you pass the harbour's south entrance.

It was still murky and cold, I had my weatherproofs on and I had food and a flask of hot soup in the cockpit but I was suddenly overwhelmed with a desire to sleep. I fought it but off Folkestone I succumbed. My hand was still on the tiller so we made progress, but when that slipped off Baladin came round into the wind and the different motion woke me up. In this state I would never make Newhaven so I decided to go to Rye, but to get to Rye you have to pass Dungeness Power Station and it won't let you. This huge hulk appeared through the mist and as one got nearer you could see it was a monstrous piece of architecture. Under normal circumstances I could have accepted that, but these were not normal circumstances. I was cold and tired and hungry and I wanted the grey forbidding mass behind me but it wouldn't shift. I slowly built up within me an intense hatred for this object which stood between me and my bunk.

After what seemed an eternity we got around it and hugged the coast at the same time keeping an eye open through the mist and the rain for the entrance to Rye. The wind had freshened up and this helped to revive one's flagging spirits but during that black period one starts to doubt oneself, regarding the wisdom of embarking on such an adventure at 'my' age. My wife's reference to Walter Mitty on my departure from home made me wonder if there was not some element of truth to it. What am I trying to do? What am I trying to prove? Who am I trying to impress? Maybe I'm getting too old, maybe I should give it all up, but then who would take care of my beloved "Baladin"? Who would have the same affection and understanding of her ways as I do? We're a good team and we've had some great times together. Sod it, all I want to do is sail and sail I bloody well will.

Having shaken myself out of this dark mood and on a point of principle I would not look back at that power station. I kept looking forward to Rye. A board sailor came by and I hailed him to enquire its whereabouts, he pointed. "It's there two hundred yards away, but be careful you're on a falling tide."

I took down the sails and carefully made my way into the narrow entrance. I headed for the pilings on the starboard side and then with no more than three yards to go we went aground. Hell and damnation this was all I needed but there was nothing to do but accept the fact that I was going to be stuck there for some considerable time.

It was 18.45, I had been at the tiller for nearly 11½ hours but my bunk and a decent night's sleep would elude me. It turned out a fine sunny evening so after I stowed everything away I sat on the cabin roof with a can of beer and a pipe of tobacco. People out walking on the other side of the river stopped to look. No one said anything but then what could they say? Any comment would have been fatuous. I consoled myself that the tide would turn and shortly after midnight I should be afloat and out of this predicament. As our angle became more acute I stretched out in the cockpit then when the tide went right out I clambered overboard and took bow and stern lines to the mooring poles. The sun had by now set and a chill night descended beneath a dark velvet coat of a million stars. I put on a reefer coat and jammed myself in the cabin. I could not open my food locker for to do so would have had the entire contents being disgorged onto the deck. I sat huddled for some considerable time willing myself to heed the philosophy I am always ready to impart to others which is "don't worry in six months' time you won't even remember it". That is a damn silly thing to say. How is it ones counsel always appears good for others but not for oneself? I dozed off in a fitful sleep dreaming of desert islands and faraway places, only to be interrupted as a clatter on deck warned me that my tobacco jar and boat hook had fallen down as we reverted to a more presentable angle. At 00.30 I finally pulled in my mooring lines and decorated the starboard side of Baladin with fenders of every shape and size, but I knew even now there would be no sleep. I would have to take up the slack as the tide rose and would the fenders be in the correct position? I did not undress but lay down for half hour periods at a time, imagining the pulpit getting caught under the horizontal timbers, or maybe the outboard getting damaged. There were creaks and groans throughout the night that played havoc with one's imagination. At 03.00 the fishing boats went out and with every passing vessel their wash slammed us against the piles and then the grinding noise, oh yes, the grinding noise. I could only be losing my rubbing strake. On investigation I found a mixture of fenders and rubbing strakes were knocking off the barnacles on the piles. Shortly after daybreak I sought out the Harbour Master and asked him whether he had a berth that didn't dry out.

"No," he said, "but if you go upstream to the Strand Quay you'll get a mud berth and the fishing boats won't disturb you."

I took his advice and as soon as I had sufficient depth of water, I motored up river. Coming alongside the Strand Quay I duly tied up. It is of course vital with a fin keel to take the necessary precautions to ensure that your vessel stays in an upright position when the tide leaves you. To this end I took the main sheet halyard, threaded it through the ladder and back to the boat. The normal mooring lines were slack enough for low tide. Then I put a line between the mooring rings ashore and from this line I attached a rope the other end being a slack bowline that would ride up and down the mast and a similar one to the back stay,

Having taken care of Baladin I decided to have a quick two hour nap and then go ashore to sample the wares of a local tavern. I did not wake up until 08.00 the next morning having not undressed for two days.

The sun was shining, the sky was blue and Baladin had gone up and down with no problems. It was not long before the peace and tranquillity of this old town took a hold on me. Why should I sweat and strain to get to the Isle of Wight. Rye has an appeal to me so here I decided to stay and forget my aspirations.

I walked a lot. I visited most of the taverns and generally enjoyed the delightful old houses, each with their own characteristics. Brick and stone and flint, old beams and stucco, ivy creeping up the walls and a wild profusion of colours bordering neatly cut lawns.

In one tavern I was foolish enough to ask the landlord what time he closed. Up to that moment he had buried his head in a newspaper only interrupted by an occasional customer, but with that question he came alive. "Eleven o'clock," he almost exploded. "The bastards asked for the extension and got it. Why do we want to stay open until eleven, you don't get any more customers, you don't sell any more beer, all you have to do is to pay more staff. Take the local newsagent he used to come in at 9.15 spend nearly three quid and go. What does he do now? Comes in at 10.15 spends nearly three quid and goes. People think this is a great life, I could tell them yes I could tell them. Do you know there are some 37 people that can claim the right to come into my pub and inspect their particular interest. There's the VAT people, the income tax, weights and measures, the health inspectors, people who check the kitchens, people who check the pipes, people who check floors and glasses and optics. Did you know I can't clean the optics?" Before I could answer he continued. "See the seal on them? I can't take them to bits. Harold Wilson did that because he claimed some publicans were putting the old sixpence in the optic and getting two extra measures a bottle as a result. They can come in and check my guests' luggage without so much as by your leave, then there's the performing rights…" He was still talking as I said goodnight and made my way back to the peace and quiet of Baladin.

The following day I took the footpath by the river and over the railway line, climbed a hill which brought me out into a cemetery then down to a pub for some refreshments, but this idyllic countryside had now to take second place to my making tracks for home. I had resolved that from now on I would be a fair-weather sailor, anything above force 1 and I would stay in harbour, but one's resolutions for a quiet life are soon forgotten and especially is that so with the pressures of time.

The day of departure arrived. It was dull, overcast and showery. The forecast was Westerly 3/4 backing south 5/6 with gale force 8 later. The winds would be with me and if the gale broke early I could seek shelter in Dover if not I would go on to Ramsgate.

I prepared a mountain of food, checked every piece of equipment on Baladin, donned my wet gear and slipped my mooring at 05.20.

Once outside the river I found the wind was from the east and merely a light breeze but at least I had the current with me. The cold penetrated one's old bones but we arrived at the power station at 07.55. The seas changed their character to that of long rolling waves. In a moment of madness I thought I would cut across the channel to Calais but with this unsettled weather I deemed it inadvisable. I had kept the engine going with the wind being on the nose and reached the Sandgate North Cardinal at 10.45. Refuelling operations were tricky but Mike bought me a hand pump last year which helped considerably. As I passed Dover at 13.00 the Harbour Patrol came out. My first reaction was what have I done wrong, but they came to exchange pleasantries and motored alongside me for ten minutes. While the first part of the weather forecast was wrong the second part was correct because the wind veered round to the south and freshened considerably. The situation had now reversed in that the tide was against me and with the wind behind increasing in intensity it made a lumpy but exhilarating sail, until that is the shackle came off the jib sheet kicking strap. This was irritating when I had so carefully checked it, however I just dropped the jib and proceeded under the main. At 16.20 we were off the West Goodwin and at 16.30 I made such a terrible hash of the refuelling that smoking was out of the question for the rest of the trip. At 18.15 we tied up in the inner harbour at Ramsgate, and to my amazement I found the offending shackle pin lying in the folds of the sail.

At 20.00 the last part of the forecast erupted into a force 8 gale, necessitating those wonderful characters of the RNLI putting to sea. I must however give credit to my little five horse power Yamaha, it went continuously for nearly 13 hours on three gallons of fuel. I have no desire to offend Baladin so will also give credit to her for being such a marvellous dependable little vessel which is a delight to sail.

I spent a few days in Ramsgate, one of which embraced a trip to Margate by bus (a place I had not visited for nearly sixty years) and then I took the Sally Line to Dunkerque with a bus trip to Bruges thrown in. I must confess I relished the comfort of the ferry, no buffeting about, no necessity for wet gear or a life belt, and for sheer luxury to be able to sit down to a decent meal. What it lacked was the personal achievement of sailing your own vessel and plotting your own course.

I also visited the Royal Temple Yacht Club in Ramsgate who made me welcome and were most hospitable.

Eventually the time came to take the last leg back to the Crouch. At 09.30 I cast off with steady rain falling, but within half an hour the sun came out. The wind was E.SE force 2 so it was going to be a slow trip. At 10.35 I reached the Longnose and could see the lightning flashing over to the west, as a result the winds increased but veered round to the N.NW. It was exceedingly dark but I was grateful that the storm passed me by.

The Tongue Sands came up at 11.40 and the wind was now a much more comfortable force 4. We went through the Edinburgh Channel and noticed another storm approaching from the South West. At 13.30 we passed Black Deep 9 and at 13.55 Barrow 7. In Middle Deep there was quite a lot of shipping so I changed course from 340 degrees to 360 degrees to avoid it, with the result that I didn't know where the hell I was. I could just make out the coastline but could not identify what part. It really could only be Clacton, however I switched on the echo sounder and found I had a mere two metres below me. In a situation such as this it pays to go back the way you came, however I realised I was over the Gunfleet Sands so took a westerly course and found the Wallett Spitway. I went through the Swin and entered the Whittaker Channel at 16.30 so we only lost a half hour. The wind eased and swung round to the South East so I had a broad reach all the way back to Wallasea arriving there at 19.30.

I must confess that trips of ten hours or more are becoming very tiring. For some time I had been toying with the idea of getting an auto helm – at least it would give one a break from the tiller.

Grounded at Rye

GALE FORCE 9 IN THE CHANNEL

G. W. SHELTON 1987

Sailors will inevitably hit bad weather at some time in their life, but no sensible sailor will invite trouble by leaving the marina in force 9 gale conditions and especially is that so in a 21 ft sloop with three ill-equipped land lubbers. The reader will have already gleaned by now that we are not talking about sensible people.

The preamble to this venture will give some indication as to the reasons.

Sometime two years ago I had spent a glorious Sunday on Lake Lanier near Atlanta, Georgia. My host Walton had hired a luxury raft with twin outboards, and we motored between the islands until we came to a picnic site where his colleagues, their spouses and children met us. The table was covered with an array of delicacies that made one's mouth water to even dwell on the subject.

It was with this in mind that I had the desire to reciprocate whenever the occasion presented itself. Unfortunately arrangements are made without the foreknowledge of weather conditions.

Gales had blown throughout Friday night the 12th September so before leaving on Saturday morning I rang the Met Office. "Gale force 9 raging from the Thames estuary to the Humber."

I made my way to the marina where Tony was to bring along Walton and Rick from Atlanta. I had no desire to disappoint my guests and the contrast between the weather they had provided for me could hardly have been more extreme.

My initial thought was to reef the main and use the storm jib, but then I decided that in these winds (about force 7 in the marina) the storm jib would suffice.

Having prepared ship my colleagues arrived. Their attire was not quite what one would expect in such inclement conditions, but allowances had to be made in that their visit to these shores was for business not sailing down the Crouch in force 7 winds so dress of the day became the Burberry while Tony wore an anorak. Someone cast doubt on the wisdom of setting forth, but the alternative was four men sitting in a smoke filled corribee cabin for four hours drinking beer.

Walton was given my golfing gear to wear, while Rick soon became aware that the British Burberry was not designed to repel buckets of cold sea water down the neck. Tony sensibly stood in the cabin so at least his trousers were dry.

There were no other vessels to contend with and we had the river to ourselves as we sped along with the wind on our beam. It is true the storm jib fought the tiller and invariably won, which suggests that a fully reefed main would have been a welcome addition.

An occasional shower with plenty of spindrift over the bows caused discomfort but did not dampen the spirits. I was a little disappointed that we didn't get gunwales awash but that fact alone was indicative of the adequacy of the precautions taken.

We turned upstream against the tide and enjoyed an exhilarating sail, back to base. The mooring of Baladin is always a tricky manoeuvre but the day's weather suggested it was going to be a nightmare. Calling all hands on deck we prepared to enter the allotted space, but to my surprise Baladin slid into position as if there was no current and no wind to contend with. My only apprehension regarding our venture was therefore unnecessary.

Whilst I would not recommend going sailing in these conditions it is still an experience that can be savoured and enjoyed.

17
Hurricane

Like most people in the South East, the high winds on Thursday 15th October, 1987 kept us awake. The following morning found widespread devastation with damaged property, fallen trees and shrubs, blocked roads, cancellation of trains and sundry other items that I will not embark on here. Suffice to say there was minimal damage to the house and the car. I could not get to work; neither could I make telephone calls though incoming calls were unaffected. I decided that I would take my wife to lunch then in the afternoon I would visit "Baladin".

About 12.30 the phone rang. It was Howard from Southminster. He had been to Burnham and witnessed a scene of devastation. The marina at Wallasea was gone. What was left of it was on the Burnham side surrounded by stricken and wrecked vessels. He had seen Baladin lying in the midst of this carnage, holed and lying on the mud.

The conversation was only interspersed with my interruptions which consisted of, "No, no that's terrible! I can't believe it!" My wife could only hear my side of the conversation, and as I replaced the phone stricken with emotion she was convinced there had been a bereavement in the family.

"It's Baladin," I said. "I must go to her."

A look of amazement adorned her face, she could not believe what she was hearing. It was like a wife suddenly finding that her husband had a mistress, and here was this emotional pathetic wreck blind to any luncheon arrangements only desperate to visit his lady love.

I ran out of the house and raced as fast as conditions would allow to Burnham.

The scene from the sea wall could only be described as maritime carnage. A vast graveyard of boats intermingled with others struggling to survive. The tide was out, but like the reaper it would soon return to clutch within its bosom any vessel which lacked the will to survive.

I made my way over the mud flats sinking past my knees with every step. I fell on my face and acquired a thick coating of vile smelling mud. My weight was an impediment to my progress but two young people came to my assistance, until eventually I reached a pontoon physically exhausted and fighting for breath.

On regaining some semblance of composure I scrambled over numerous vessels lying against or on each other. Some would never sail again. Climbing over these boats was like climbing over tombstones in a cemetery. It was wrong but it had to be. Intermingled with those vessels were the remnants of the marina with angle irons twisted into grotesque shapes.

At length I found Baladin. She had a hole in the bow, stanchions were bent, canvas dodgers were in shreds, her rubbing strake was smashed and the outboard bracket was bent. I went below and could find no trace of water, the bilges were dry so that was a bonus. I then pondered on Malcolm Rigg's boat "Beatrice". She had been moored in the stream where the marina now was, I looked for her without success and could only assume she had been engulfed, I turned back to Baladin and saw Howard and Sue on the river bank. Howard came over to give me a hand but there was so little we could do. We tied her more firmly to the remnants of the pontoons and I decided to spend the night aboard. Howard went back and I pondered my decision. Baladin was trapped on the inside of a huge letter O.

The circle had a small gap in it which was being obstructed by a sunken yacht and two sunken launches. If the marina or what was left of it floated when the tide came in, Baladin could be crushed. If it didn't float it would take Baladin down with it. I decided it would be unwise to stay aboard, but temporary repairs had to be made. I cut a square out of the remnants of the canvas dodgers and tied it round the hole in the bow. From the inside a plastic bag full of rags was stuffed into the hole. The anchor chain was then piled against it. Every available fender was brought into use. Sadly I left Baladin not knowing what the future held for her.

Making my way back across the mud flats I saw Malcolm on the bank. Once again I got stuck with mud filling my wellington boots. Fortunately Malcolm threw me a huge mooring buoy which I was able to lay on while I extricated my feet. It was raining, blowing hard and miserable but at least I was on terra firma. Malcolm and I exchanged footwear and by using a block of polystyrene Malcolm positively skied over the mud to look for "Beatrice". Eventually he returned to say he had found her wedged between the outside of the marina and lying on two sunken boats.

We returned to Malcolm's weekend caravan and his wife Maureen. The caravan had also been damaged, but the priority now was to beat the tide. Malcolm borrowed a dinghy and some oars and together we headed out to "Beatrice". The tide would reach her first. The first thing to do was to pump the water out. The forward hatch cover had disappeared and we supposed she had shipped half the ocean through there. Damage appeared minimal, however as soon as the tide was high enough we were able to reverse out and tie up to a buoy in the stream. We had broken one of the oars nevertheless in a clumsy manner we paddled to Baladin who was now afloat. Suddenly the thought of saving her became a reality. We were unaware at the time but the outboard engine bracket was severely damaged so if we could get the engine going and if we had enough water beneath us we could escape from the O. It was now dark and we both were cold, wet, tired and hungry. After some coaxing the engine sprang to life, slowly we edged forward. We avoided the forestay of the sunken yacht but hit another obstruction below us. We reversed and the screw hit a twisted girder. I thought the sheer pin had snapped but no, we moved forward. Somehow Baladin was not responding as she should. I was not to know her rudder was about 10 degrees off the vertical so thought it was the weight distribution. I had moved everything aft to keep the bows out of the water.

Wallasea was in darkness due to the power failure but we called out into the blackness of the night. "Are you taking any boats out?"

"Only those that are holed,' came the reply.

"We are holed."

We pulled in alongside another boat pending the haul out, but then when the time came the engine would not work. I do not know how the marina staff managed to manoeuvre that huge machine in the dark but they did and soon a bedraggled looking "Baladin" was safely ashore.

It was now nearly 2130 and both Malcolm's and my car were the other side of the river. A motor boat kindly offered to tow the dinghy but nearing the wrecks he hit an underwater obstruction. They restarted the engine only to stall again when a life belt became entangled in the propeller. Another boat came to their rescue while Malcolm and I paddled off into the darkness.

When I arrived home at 2300 the house was in darkness, my wife was asleep. I peeled off my vile smelling mud caked clothes and dropped then into the bath after which I proceeded to wash them. Four changes of water could not conceal the terrible aroma that pervaded the house.

On Saturday I learnt from Malcolm that Beatrice was more severely damaged than we had supposed and it was only through the astuteness of Tucker Brown's Yard who perceived she was taking water and took the necessary measures to save her from a watery grave.

In retrospect I think that both Malcolm and I were hasty in thinking that all the water aboard could have come in through the forward hatch, further laying against the tangled marina wreck on one side and two sunken launches supporting her on the other side. It really was unbelievable that we could have supposed her injuries were minimal. As Malcolm said later, weather conditions prevailing at the time allied to cold, tiredness, hunger and physical exhaustion were not conducive to clear thinking.

Considering the number of larger boats that had been sunk or severely damaged, this experience is once again testimony to the quality and strength that goes into the construction of this wonderful little vessel, the Corribee.

Both "Beatrice" and "Baladin" will soon recover to their former glory, and both look to and anticipate more adventures in the year to come.

1 8
Odds and Ends

Life is not all about sailing, in fact just being in the marina can have its hairy moments, so the following are a few odds and ends between voyages.

The time is January and my wife and I are sitting in our old armchairs in front of a redbrick fireplace which contains a huge log fire. Outside a cold north east wind blows across the Essex lowlands and swirls around the old homestead dusting it with snowflakes. A draught beneath a badly fitting door produces a low hum. The wife is absorbed by a book whilst I am draped in sails and other nautical paraphernalia. The spare bedroom has been converted to a temporary winter sail storage loft, while down below with clumsy fingers encased in a sail maker's palm I attempt to sew on new ties to the sail cover, and make new nettings for the guard rails and to carefully check over the sails.

Whilst feverishly engaged in this labour of love I become conscious that my wife was looking at me. As I looked up she said, "You must be mad." Not once has she complained about the bedroom, not once has she commented in an adverse manner about the nightly mess on the sitting room floor.

It is true that she drops a barbed hint about the house falling to bits for lack of care, so I make a mental note to achieve the necessary redecorating before the spring arrives.

There is no doubt that sewing is very relaxing and allows one's mind to wander without having to concentrate on the task in hand. It allows one to indulge in flights of fancy or should one say sails of fancy. A fair breeze, a warm day, a beautiful sea and sails full of wind to take you wherever you wish. It was a logical progression of thought to think of Baladin still afloat in the marina, and my conscience pricked me that I hadn't seen her for three weeks.

I decided that I must visit her over the weekend but no sooner had these thoughts come into my mind when I realised my wife was looking at me as though she knew what I was thinking. It brought me back to the wretched decorating problem so I resolved to buy the paint on Saturday morning and then visit Baladin: in that way it would appease or please both ladies.

**

Following my winter activities I was eager to fit the new netting. The day chosen for this was memorable because Dick from Chicago was to come sailing with me the following day, so one might say why should this be so special, and the answer is that very few people have chosen to sail with me a second time, so Dick either has a very bad memory or our American cousins are madder than I had imagined, but to get back to the netting, this has to be thought out very carefully. It is not as simple a task as one would suppose it to be, for example you take one netting at a time leaving the other below in case it falls overboard. Make sure it is the correct way up and make up your mind where to start top, bottom, forward or aft. I unravelled the cord and decided to start top aft. From here on out it is easy, a clove hitch round the stanchion and I'm on my way, hold it something's jammed - ah yes I'm sitting on it. Lift left cheek and proceed but she won't shift. I then notice a loop around my right foot. I kick it off making sure I am not sitting on anything or kicking anything, next loop through and damn me it's caught again, what now oh yes caught round the capstan, I unfree but not for long this time there's a double turn round a cleat. I decide to throw the loose end into the cabin it won't get into trouble there, but it does its now jammed under the hatch. To add to this I have a north wind blowing up my jumper and I am short of breath with bending over my paunch and now I'm short of temper, but resist the temptation to explode into obscene vulgarities as I have given up blasphemy for Lent, but the next thing is the netting gets caught in the bottle screws, and then I find I'm sitting in a wet patch. When I finally accomplish my task I find the cord (which is the same one I used last year) is too short. With this realisation plus the fact I recall Lent finished over a week ago, I gave vent to my feelings in a rather verbally expressive way. Of one thing I am sure, no sailor would ever have conceived the idea of 'Sod's Law'.

When I arrived home the phone rang, it was Dick. "You sound far off Dick. Where are you ringing from?"

"Chicago," came the reply. "I've had to delay the trip." Now was that Sod's Law or Dick having second thoughts, or his wife being overprotective.

Throughout Saturday night sixty and seventy mile an hour gales blew down the east coast and well into Sunday morning; when I went down to the marina I was going to move Baladin to another berth no more than a half cable's length away but decided against it. However whilst pondering the problem I heard an engine starting up. I thought it rather foolish for anyone to be going out in weather like this when I realised that although they had cast off the wind was so strong their boat was jammed against the finger of the pontoon. I went to assist by standing on a motor boat the other side of the finger. I remember thinking how stable she was for such a small boat because my weight had absolutely no effect on her. I had of course failed to realise that it was the pressure of the other boat that was keeping the one I was on so stable so that when I managed to free it, mine keeled over at an alarming angle, my foot hold was barely four inches and there were no grab rails to hold onto merely a canvas cockpit cover. I couldn't move without falling into the water. If only someone would come along and stand on the other side of the boat I would be alright, I pondered on the idea of falling in to get out of this predicament but the trouble with falling in is getting the contents of your pockets and wallet dry. I hung on for fifteen minutes when I heard a voice behind me, "Are you alright?"

I dared not look behind but said, "I am now that you have arrived."

19
Levington

The Corribee Owners Association had arranged a rally at Levington Marina on the River Orwell which meant that if one was going to attend then it would be wise to allow more than two days. With this in mind Malcolm and his son David would in "Beatrice" accompany Baladin and I to the rally and use the trip for our annual holiday, and so one evening I motored from Wallasea to mooring on the Burnham side of the Crouch where I tied up to a buoy just astern of "Beatrice". This was the first time that both vessels had been together since they were stricken on the night of the hurricane nine months previously. It was a pleasant warm evening with an occasional burst of sunshine through the low lying clouds.

At 19.00 Malcolm and his son arrived to provision ship and when this had been accomplished they rowed over to Baladin armed with a bottle of whisky with the purpose of discussing our departure the following day.

Our first port of call was intended to be Brightlingsea where we would meet Colin aboard "Roaring Forties" and sail in company to the River Orwell.

David who is 17 did not appear to capture the spirit of his two elderly colleagues, but was rather more concerned that he was going to miss a performance by some character called Michael Jackson. Having checked times and tides and marked out our course Malcolm and David retired to spend the night in their caravan.

I watched their departure with some amusement as the two sets of oars were not in harmony causing the dinghy to take a very erratic course. The skipper soon restored order by confining his crew to sit idly in the bow. A fleeting thought passed through my mind that young David is no fool (except of course in his choice of music).

There was consistent rain throughout the night and the 06.00 shipping forecast predicted southerly winds 4 rising 5-7 later. I didn't like the 7 part but hopefully we would be in Brightlingsea before it manifested itself.

Both vessels slipped their moorings at 10.15 and we had reached the mouth of the Roach by 11.05. Twenty minutes later disaster hit us as Beatrice's roller reefing collapsed, the shackle holding it to the top of the mast having broken. There was no alternative but to abort the trip and return to our moorings.

Malcolm had to take the mast down but after three hours the problem was resolved and the trip would then start the following day.

We proposed leaving at 10.00 with the object of going over the Ray Sands. Regrettably the weather was atrocious and the wind so fierce that we deferred our departure. At 11.00 it was just as bad however by 13.30 there was a slight improvement so we decided to go. With this loss of time we had lost the opportunity of going over the Ray and we were therefore obliged to take the longer route through the Swin but we did of course have the ebb tide with us, which helped our speed considerably. We arrived at the Spitway at 16.00 but with the last of the ebb tide and the N.W. wind against us our progress was minimal. Malcolm called over with the suggestion that we forget Brightlingsea and take advantage of the wind on our port beam and head for Walton. This was a good move though we had no means of contacting Colin to inform him of the change of plan.

An exhilarating sail combined with winds of increasing intensity allowed us to speed along the coast past Clacton, Frinton and Walton. Beatrice was way ahead of me and barely discernible in the descending gloom. I decided to start up the outboard to catch him up but conditions were so rough it proved impossible, but having passed the Medusa buoy it became obvious that Malcolm was not going to Walton. A quick check of the chart suggested that rather than backtrack it would be easier to carry on to Harwich.

I arrived in the harbour at 20.00 only to find "Beatrice" had engine problems so I took her in tow until we reached a mooring buoy just south of Shotley Point. Conditions were so rough we decided to look for a more comfortable mooring in the lee of the land. Malcolm rowed over and together we found some visitors mooring buoys just to the east of Shotley Point. We then went back to Beatrice and towed her to calmer waters. When she was tied up I cast off but regrettably the tail of a rope caught round my screw with the result that it broke the sheer pin leaving me adrift in Harwich harbour with no engine and no sails up. After a few anxious moments I drifted up alongside a moored sea going tug and managed to get a line round its anchor chain. His steel bows were higher than Baladin's mast which gave me considerable cause for concern but the problem now was to put in a new sheer pin. I still had Malcolm's dinghy tied up astern but when I observed its cubic capacity and my bulk I decided it would be preferable to remove the engine rather than trust myself to the tender.

At 21.30 with the problem rectified I tied up to the mooring buoy. Malcolm came over with the scotch and recognising how insensitive it would have been not to imbibe we settled down to enjoy the best part of our journey so far with all our troubles behind us. At least that is what we thought at the time.

Our moorings did not turn out as comfortable as we had supposed but the important thing was to tidy up our boats, dry our wet clothes and get ashore. Having been on board for three days I had plenty of rubbish to take ashore and also needed a shower.

The following day we made our way up the Orwell to Levington marina where I had to take Beatrice in tow as the engine was still out of action. David made some comment about not being accustomed to seeing Baladin's stern. While there was more than an element of truth in his utterances I noticed he was wise enough to refrain from echoing such thoughts until Beatrice was safely tucked up in the marina.

Adjourning to the Yacht Club which is in fact an old lightship, we met up with other Corribeer's and received news that we had been missing for two days. Colin had rung up to say he was coming by road as it was too rough but in fact he did sail in after dark.

These annual events held at various locations around the country present wonderful opportunities to see other members and their boats from which we all draw ideas. Over the weekend we sail in company and enjoy a communal pub lunch with a get together in a local restaurant in the evening.

On the Monday I crewed for Malcolm as we accompanied those vessels making the homeward trek. Ron on "Kotuku II" very kindly lent his seagull outboard to Malcolm whilst his was getting repaired.

Malcolm is one of those characters that is constantly fiddling. His boat is full of odds and ends which may come in useful. Each time he gets into the marina he either empties the lazarette or the cabin. Everything is piled into the cockpit. There are of course things you expect such as fenders and fuel cans and shackles but Malcolm has an excess of equipment, a bucketful of shackles and odds and ends. There are pulleys and electrical equipment, there is a storm lantern and a 130' roll of one inch manila. There is a spare anchor and a huge expanding riveter which may come in handy. The list is endless but it attracts the attention of passers-by who think a boat sale is in progress. When everything is put back he then makes a start in the cabin. This ritual is a daily event to which other marina users become accustomed.

Soon the time arrived to leave Levington and so with a west wind and an ebb tide we departed at 09.15. We were off Landguard Point at 10.20 and Woodbridge E Haven at 11.45 and then we reached the mouth of the Deben. There is always a certain apprehension about entering this river as the sand banks are allegedly constantly on the move. One is in fact advised to enter on a low tide in order that you may quite clearly see the obstacles which may impede your progress. We were just past the bottom of the tide and while it is advisable to follow someone who looks as though they know the way in we did not have that luxury so the alternative was to watch the boats coming out.

Baladin led the way making a direct line at right angles to the beach. About thirty yards from the shore you make a hard 90 degree turn to starboard and follow the line of the beach. Even at low tide you can see on your starboard hand an angry turmoil of whirlpools and eddies.

Getting into the Deben is like prizing open a precious jewel case but once inside she reveals herself in all her glory. Although reasonably broad her navigable channel is narrow and twists and turns to such an extent that every quarter of the boat is exposed at some time to the wind. The beautiful Suffolk hills gently roll down to the water's edge, while the boats follow the buoys in the ribbon of meandering water. It is not a river to take liberties in but no harm will come to you if you do. Malcolm decided to cut a corner at Woldringfield and went around, but he was on a rising tide and the half hour he had to wait was profitably used in the preparation of a meal.

This used to scare Malcolm when the waters poured into the cockpit

We reached Woodbridge Marina by 14.30 and being of a lesser draught were able to enter over the bar before some of the bigger boats.

The term marina conjures up in the mind a sophisticated boat park with top class facilities, showers, chandlery and a yacht club, but there are marinas and marinas and Woodbridge forms part of the latter. I do not criticise it in an adverse manner for that. It takes the shape of a horseshoe the entrance being at the bottom. It certainly has showers in fact I have never seen individual showers so large, and the pontoons could not be described as modern yet on the other hand they are serviceable and are not out of place in this lovely old town. Woodbridge is a very attractive place that could easily seduce me into retiring there except of course for the low flying American Air Force planes which constantly take one by surprise. There are so many old wooden boats adorning the water front that you could easily believe you were in a time warp.

Malcolm rang his wife Maureen thinking that with the aid of the car he could return the borrowed engine to Levington and pick up his own which was now in Brightlingsea. I hardly dare conjecture on Maureen's thoughts but she obligingly came down and stayed the night.

Our holiday was coming to an end and it was time to make tracks for home so on the Friday night at the height of the tide we left Woodbridge and motored downstream where we spent the night moored off of Ramsholt, in order that we might make an early start in the morning.

The weather is no respecter of beautiful rivers which was made evident with the force 5/6 winds which blew throughout the night.

They maintained their strength the following morning and coming from the S.W. meant it was going to be a long hard haul back to the Crouch.

We slipped our moorings at 08.10 and exited the river at 0900, we did not however expect the Deben to so discourteously throw us out in the manner she did.

With the main sheet reefed, a storm jib and the engine going full out our departure was spectacular. Mountainous seas confronted us as high as our yard arms, one moment we were going up at a 45 degree angle and then we slid down into the troughs. If our journey was going to be like this it would be better to abort the trip, but even if those thoughts entered our minds there was no way we could turn back. In fact the thought did not occur to us for the simple reason we were too preoccupied with trying to control our respective vessels to think of anything else; then it suddenly ceased and soon we were in more comfortable waters. When I use the expression more comfortable it is done in a comparative form for conditions were still exceedingly rough and unpleasant with that force 5 to 6 bang on the nose.

Baladin had been nagging me for some time to purchase an auto helm. She felt it would give me a break from the tiller on long journeys, so I duly indulged her, but due to a large girth I had not been able to get into the quarter berth to fit the necessary attachments. Fortunately David who is somewhat slimmer kindly obliged me when we were at Woodbridge and now I was presented with my first opportunity to try it out. I soon found that in these heavy seas and sailing close to the wind one could soon lose control but bearing away from the wind a few points made life more comfortable and so for the first time in our association I was able to sit back with my arms folded. Somehow it didn't seem right so I decided to go into the cabin to investigate the source of the noise I had been listening to. Of course it was chaos below but barely had I put foot to cabin deck when I went base over apex. The cap to the washing up liquid container had come off and it was all over the deck. I tried to clean it up but wringing deck cloths out saturated in liquid soap was like trying to mop up engine oil, and then I saw bubbles coming out of the bilges, billowing up and going down with every motion of the boat. As I clambered out of the cabin I noticed the jib sheet had caught round a cleat on the mast, so with the auto helm still working I took the precaution of tying myself to Baladin. I went forward forgetting that the soles of my shoes were covered in liquid soap, with the result that standing on the port side adjacent to the mast my feet slipped under the guard rails and my legs up to the knees went in the water. For once my bulk worked in my favour and prevented me from going all the way through.

It soon became apparent that we would never make the Crouch so when "Beatrice" and "Baladin" came within hailing distance Malcolm and I agreed to go to Harwich and on to Levington Marina.

I had disconnected the auto helm with the object of getting closer to the wind but found great difficulty in going about.

Progress was slow so I decided to get the outboard going, well she started alright but I could not get it into gear so there was no alternative but to do it the hard way. I had not realised it at the time but the tail of a coil of rope I keep in the cockpit had washed overboard and jammed itself around the screw and broken the shear pin.

At 13.45 I entered Harwich and at 15.00 I sailed into Levington having taken nearly seven hours for a twelve mile trip, meanwhile Malcolm's repaired engine was playing up and when he checked it he found so many loose parts it was a wonder it had not disintegrated at sea.

Back in Levington we met other seafarers whose plans had embraced going to the continent and places north and south along the coast but the foul weather had kept them all in harbour. With our respective engines repaired we planned to leave on Sunday morning but the forecast was still S.W. winds but ranging from 6 to gale force. Whilst one accepts that putting to sea in a 21 ft sloop with gales forecast is inadvisable, the biggest deterrent was the continuous S.W. winds.

Monday arrived and there was still no let up so as we both had jobs to go to we left our vessels and returned home by rail.

The following Friday night we arrived at the marina to prepare for our trip home. Again we saw the same faces at Levington as the entire week had been just a continuation of the previous one. We still couldn't go on Saturday but Sunday morning dawned with clear blue skies. I was awake at 05.00 and prepared Baladin for sea. Apart from the snoring all was quiet aboard "Beatrice." I listened to the shipping forecast which reported S.W. winds (again) 5 to 6 decreasing 4 to 5 later. I listened to the forecast and observed the weather overhead: there was no comparison.

I banged on "Beatrice's" cabin and yelled out, "We're going." Malcolm and David were awake but still in their bunks and I wondered if they sensed a lack of conviction in my voice. Soon there was a flurry of activity, showers, shaving and breakfast were dispensed with in their feverish efforts to prepare Beatrice. I must confess that I hoped that this sudden and early departure would allow us to get a few miles behind us before adverse weather set in.

We cast off at 06.40 and had a pleasant sail down the Orwell. I went aground making a short cut at the entrance to Harwich harbour but managed to get off surprisingly quickly. The time was now 07.30 and we set a course for the Medusa buoy which we reached at 09.35.

It soon became apparent that the forecast was more reliable than my prediction. The wind was still on the nose force 5 to 6. I could not use the auto helm, the gunwales were under the water half the time and periodically the ocean decided to see what the inside of the cockpit looked like. There were indeed times when it was coming in faster than it was draining out. Baladin was wearing a storm jib and an unreefed main and I had set a course that would take me over the Gunfleet Sands. I saw Beatrice taking a more coastal route but she turned and was travelling almost parallel to Baladin. Visibility was not very good and I lost sight of Malcolm. At 11.50 I reached the South Whitaker but yearned to get into the Crouch and out of these rough seas.

I started the outboard as I wanted to make the most of the tide but after five minutes it cut out. I tried again a half hour later but the same thing happened. My spirits went down a notch, soon I would have to battle both tide and wind and this would take forever. The other opportunities open to me were either to drop anchor on the edge of the sands and wait for the tide to turn, or to cut across the Ray Sands with the wind on my port quarter and spend the night in Brightlingsea. I did not favour the former and it is doubtful whether there was sufficient water on the Ray at this state of the tide. There was another alternative: I offered up a prayer following which I tried the engine again. She never faltered. I kept my sails up as added insurance and immediately felt ashamed at my lack of faith so I removed them.

Arriving back in the Crouch I headed for Beatrice's mooring but there was no sign of her. Malcolm's boat is faster than Baladin so he should have arrived first but did he by chance elect to go to Brightlingsea? As this jumble of thoughts flitted through my mind I heard a familiar voice, it was Malcolm. He too had had engine trouble and had chosen to pick up the first available mooring.

I tied up in the marina at 16.30 having taken nearly ten hours for the trip. I was wet, tired and hungry, unkempt and dishevelled. Malcolm and Sandra who own "Toto" helped me tie up. They had missed Baladin and were getting anxious as to our whereabouts. Sandra then made me a cup of tea, and will never know how good it tasted and then she cleaned my salt rimmed glasses. The depth of the welcome home made the ordeal that much more bearable.

I went into the cabin to clear up and darn me the liquid soap was up to its tricks again only this time my cap was lying upside down in the middle of it. A water container had also broken so I now have the cleanest bilges in the river, though I must say it looked most odd, for when I used the bilge pump and all this soapy water came out occasionally you would get this huge bubble which mockingly rose up and burst in your face.

In future I will believe the forecasters and will elect for a quiet life, anything over force 1 and I stay in harbour and if it's from the S.W. I won't even go aboard.

Pin Mill, Ipswich

20
Other Boats

Consorting with other boats is not something I usually discuss in front of Baladin as she does not approve, but occasionally other skippers invite me to join them in races. This is not because I have any expertise that they can tap or indeed any experience of the rules and regulations of racing. You will therefore appreciate that I am under no illusion when I tell you that it is my 17 stones that they believe is the necessary ingredient between winning and losing. Why they still maintain this optimism I know not because they have never won a race with me aboard. The idea is for me to hang over the windward side in a force 5 and above, and when it is one and below I'm hanging over the lee side. I hardly dare speculate what their intentions are between 2 and 4 but maybe that is when I do not receive an invitation.

I was therefore invited by Richard and Terry to join them on the Sunday morning in their very smart and fast "Limbo Ace". They were going to sleep aboard Saturday night to ensure they could move their berth whilst they still had sufficient water beneath them. I had elected to spend the night at home which was a wise move seeing that I had had a somewhat heavy evening added to which a storm had raged all night long. With my wife's assistance I was up by 06.00 and down the marina by 07.00 only to find "Limbo Ace" deserted. The padlock was still on so obviously they had not slept aboard.

Very soon Richard arrived and said that Terry had rung him the previous evening and expressed the view that the gale would mean the race would be cancelled. I referred Richard to the activity taking place in the marina which suggested the race was very much on. Now I should explain here that Terry is deemed to be the expert on setting the sails, while Richard is the expert where the engine is concerned so with this knowledge and Terry's absence Richard posed the question as to whether we should participate. I quickly agreed and then he said, "If you handle the canvas I'll take care of the tiller."

Now this may sound reasonable but "Limbo Ace" has so many sheets and ropes and odds and ends it is sometimes hard to know what the sheet you are pulling actually does.

We put a reef in the main and prepared the No. 2 genoa.

I asked Richard if he knew the course and he said, "No but if we move from here and tie up on the outer pontoon I will acquire it." We therefore cast off but when we attempted to come alongside the outer pontoons the wind was so strong it would have smashed us to pieces. We therefore went out into the stream and tied up to a mooring buoy, Richard then said he would get the course by W.T. from the start boat but all his endeavours went unanswered due to the fact he didn't know the name of the start boat, we were therefore reduced to calling out for details from the other participants. I then had a brilliant idea: our mooring buoy was 50 yards behind the start line and I suggested that as all our previous starts had been disastrous we could, when the gun went, slip our mooring and be in an advantageous position. Richard countered this with the thought that it was against the rules. Not being a racing man I was not in a position to contradict him so prudence prevailed, and we slipped our mooring line and headed at an oblique angle away from the start line. Unfortunately the gun went off with us being the only vessel facing the wrong way. We had to get out of the way fairly sharply and the only direction open to us was through the moorings and still away from the start. The next thing was a huge gin palace was moored just where we wanted to go. Without wishing to apportion blame the crew were divided as to whether we should pass it astern or across the bows. The latter view prevailed with the result that we ended up with a bent stanchion and a torn dodger. Our exploits were however to continue. We were on a lee shore and we had not recovered any modicum of speed after the fracas with the motor boat thereby denying us the opportunity to gybe before the current drove us aground.

I rushed below to raise the keel and then went forward shouting to Richard to start the engine put it in full reverse then I would run aft and we'd be away. In retrospect it was a ludicrous suggestion. I haven't run for well over 40 years and to suggest I could accelerate my weight in a small boat in heavy seas is like something out of Laurel and Hardy, however be that as it may I ambled somewhat awkwardly and clumsily (though I hasten to add there was a modicum of speed) and surprise surprise it worked!

We mutually agreed that if we tied up to a buoy we could put a reef in the main. I might add here that the racing fleet was out of sight but we were not going to be denied. Having fixed the reef we hoisted the sail with the object of sailing away from the buoy, but the next thing that happened was all the clips slipped out of the runner and the main sheet was flapping at a 90 degree angle from the top of the mast. It was obvious that without Terry we were wasting our time so in one voice we said, "Sod it, break out the beer."

It is always prudent to avoid disclosing mishaps of this nature if such mishap has escaped the attention of others. Regrettably we discovered later that there were witnesses to this strange behaviour, one of which was Terry who unbeknown to us had missed the boat and had watched our gyrations (or was it geriatric antics) from the pontoon, I also suspect that Baladin had seen me board "Limbo Ace" and put the mockers on it.

I have also sailed on Lake Michigan following which the skipper sold his boat. I have likewise sailed in San Francisco Bay and not long after that the owner retired. Then I organised the hire of a Thames Barge but the crew mutinied and when they threatened to make the skipper walk the plank, well the least said about that the better.

In this last year I have tended to alternate with Malcolm on "Beatrice" but the consequences of the arrangement are yet to be experienced.

21
Brightlingsea – by "Baladin"

Excuse me for interrupting but the Master has been doing all the talking and it's about time I told you a thing or two about him. He has certain characteristics which reveal his next move. For example when he starts to restock his beer locker it's a sure sign we are going places, though past experience has taught me not to count on getting there.

Did I tell you he had taken out the washing facilities and turned the cavity into a beer locker, but then he had to have another sink put in so I guess there must have been complaints. But I digress, three days in succession he arrived on board loaded with supplies and all of them rattled.

I soon gleaned that we were going to Brightlingsea and Malcolm with "Beatrice" would accompany us. The day of departure arrived and Beatrice came over from the new Burnham Marina to join us at Wallasea, but she came in at such a rate of knots that the inevitable was bound to happen. The Master leapt onto the pontoon (that's not quite true he is incapable of leaping) he ambled onto the pontoon in an attempt to stop Beatrice but alas even his weight could not stop her from damaging her bows.

I did not think, in fact I could not bring myself to believe that the Crouch had two idiots and yet here was Beatrice and I entrusting ourselves into their incapable hands. Beatrice was duly repaired and at 12.45 on a lovely sunny day with a westerly wind of force 2 to 3 and an ebb tide we set sail. Conditions could not be better.

At 13.00 we had the auto helm on, by 13.10 we had passed the mouth of the Roach and by 14.50 we were at the South Buxey. The Master had been warned that at the entrance to the Whittaker Channel the sands had shifted and though it was not reflected on the chart caution should be exercised. For once in his life he heeded that advice but only just. No more than fifty yards ahead the waves were breaking over what could only be shallow ground. Both Beatrice and I went hard a starboard, the engines sprang to life and we got well away. Keeping to the deeper waters we reached the Swin Spitway at 16.00. The tide had now changed so we were able to take advantage of it as we sailed into the Colne. Brightlingsea was reached by 18.15. The journey was pleasant but uneventful, in fact I cannot recall ever having made a trip without some misfortune falling upon us one way or another. I give the Master no credit for this but even he should have some good luck some time.

It goes without saying that we had gone to Brightlingsea for a rally and it was attended by numerous boats up and down the coast. I had hoped he would for my sake show a little dignity but no, one of the other skippers produced a few bottles of alcoholic sustenance and it drew him with the others like bees round a honey pot. The atmosphere became very friendly and noisy as raucous voices broke out into what they thought were expressions of musical harmony. They will never learn. He came back to me with a sickly grin adorning the makings of a brewer's face, and then he was offered a lift ashore in a rubber dinghy. If you can imagine a hippopotamus performing this same evolution you will get an idea of what it is like. Frankly I just turn my head away and pretend I have no association with him.

On the Monday preparations were made for the return trip. Malcolm decided to leave Beatrice at Brightlingsea and crew for the Master after which he would pick up his son and together they would take Beatrice up the coast, which is all very interesting but doesn't help me. What on earth have I done to deserve this!

The wind continued to be 2/3 westerly but now the sun hid behind banks of clouds. We kept company with Ron on Kotuku II as far as the Bench Head. He was going up the Blackwater while we were going over the Ray Sands.

On reaching the Crouch the winds livened up considerably and veered to the N.W. Whilst this was taking place Malcolm was in the cabin trying to pour out some coffee. He was just about to hand it to the Master when the seas just flowed into the cockpit.

"Let the main sheet go!" yelled the crew.

"No," says the Master, "just pass the coffee."

It took us just over six and a half hours to get home but really nothing went wrong. I just cannot believe it.

WHAT'S IN A NAME

By BALADIN

Is there nothing sacred? As soon as the Master read Jeremy Greenaway's article in the Autumn magazine entitled "Figitus" I knew he couldn't wait to get in on the act, and tell you all about me. Well this time I will forestall him and give you the plain truth without any embellishment and without resorting to poetic licence as an excuse to embroider the facts.

"Tell me," said the Master to the previous owner, "where did the name Baladin come from?"

"That is very interesting," came the reply. "It came about this way. I used to be married to a very beautiful French lady. I bought this Corribee just before we were divorced. I said to my wife what should I call her? To which she replied, call her Baladin. And pray what does that mean? Well, she said, in the old French it meant one who went from town to town bearing the news, but in the modern French it means a sailor's walk. So that is how Baladin acquired her name."

The Master walked away with a sense of smug satisfaction, he liked the ring to the name, and the fact it had been influenced by a very pretty French lady gave a certain added spice, however on returning home he referred to Kettridges French Dictionary, and what did it say there merely that the meaning of "BALADIN" is "CLOWN" and "BUFFOON". Now I know which half of the relationship had the last laugh, nevertheless I have been saddled with this name for some considerable time but it is only fitting that it should also adequately describe the Master.

It has however had its uses. About four years ago we sailed down the Dunkerque Roads towards Calais. The engine had ceased to function which meant that he had to rely on me. As you all know Calais is very busy and they hoist various signals to let you know when you can come in and when you must stay out. Obviously a ferry or a tanker going in and out takes priority and the small boats have to wait. Failure to heed these signals brings forth a blast on the loud speakers which leaves the recipient in no doubt regarding the Harbour Master's feelings.

The small boats were milling around with engines running and sails all down except for one – me. I was wearing a storm jib. The signal came to enter harbour but by the time I arrived at the entrance the signal said "keep out". There was no way we could comply. A noise from astern soon indicated the arrival of a ferry, but what do we do? If we keep to port we will be between the ferry and the terminal. If we go to starboard he will take our wind and his wash will put us on the rocks so what does the Master do, he stays on a middle course, ignores the glares of the Harbour Master and is thankful the loud speakers remain silent, but then having read my name they also knew what it meant.

THE WAVE

The sea is rarely constant and this is never more true than when it reaches gale force proportions. The huge rollers race across the sea with the thunder of an express train, they reach a peak that breaks into foam and then collapses only for the next wave to come and overtake them.

Whatever the wind force may be, there is always one wave that is bigger than the rest. You look out for it, you wait for it, you respect it, suddenly you see it on the starboard bow no more than two hundred yards away, you turn your bows into it and wait. As she gets nearer your bows rise, for some inexplicable reason you find yourself sliding up hill, above you a huge white crest opens its arms to embrace you, but at that very moment when you emerge from the lee side of the wave your sails become exposed to the winds, they snatch you out of the wave's grasping arms and then slam you down. The downward descent is like a slow motion film. Although your boat is at an angle of 45° your mast is in fact parallel to the wave. You do not go downhill in the same manner you went up, the wind has seen to that, for you are going down sideways, beam on and falling like a lift out of control. Slowly your boat comes to the vertical, leaving in the side of the wave a series of white streaks. The noise almost disappears as you come to a gentle halt in what is a temporary oasis of tranquillity. It is like being at the bottom of a huge basin and knowing that sooner or later you are going to be ejected. The wind bounces off the sides of the basin, but without the strength of its cousins above. Your sails flap uncontrollably, not knowing what is expected of them.

There is a way out, but you have very little to do with it. Point your nose into the side and wait for the upsurge. With the knuckles on the tiller-hand showing white, you make your ascent, leaving further white streaks in the walls behind you. A quick glance astern and you observe the relative calmness of the trough you have just left. The wave breaks before you reach the peak, suggesting you have just sailed through a waterfall, barely do you recover from this drenching when the wind catches your sails and slams you over.

Have you made progress? You don't know. Did you slip back? It could be. Are you on the right course? Maybe, at least for some of the time – and that is just one wave.

22
Havengore – by "Baladin"

I have undertaken to write this account for the reason that the Master would either be too embarrassed to write it himself or in the alternative would leave it out entirely.

Now the Corribeers in the Medway were going to hold their first rally and Malcolm and you know who thought it would be a nice idea to go and support them. Neither of them relished the idea of going all the way around the Foulness Sands so the alternative was to go through Havengore and save themselves a few hours. Before undertaking this trip it is necessary to take certain precautions. Once through the bridge you have to cross the firing range so the first task was to ring the Range Operations Officer. He said that they don't fire on Saturdays and rarely before nine o'clock. I imagine that potential invaders should be warned not to invade on a Saturday. He then rang the Bridge Keeper to ensure that the bridge would open. He was told it would but was at the same time warned that we were on neap tides. "How much do you draw?" asked the Keeper.

"About a metre and a quarter," replied the Master.

"And what is that in real language?" said the Keeper.

"About four feet," was the reply.

"You won't make it," said the Keeper. "You can get through the bridge but you'll never make it over the bar."

The Master listened attentively and was a little disappointed at what he had heard. Now two days before the trip he had some builders working on his house and mentioned the problem to them. "Don't worry," they said, "we've been through there dozens of times. Never had a problem. What size boat did you say 21 ft, yes she'll do it easy."

On Friday night we motored over to Burnham Marina to discuss the problem with Malcolm. The alternative was to catch the ebb tide, leave at midnight and go the long way round, but there was a weakness, these two old codgers needed their sleep and after all builders should know about these things so Havengore it was to be.

At 07.30 we slipped out of the marina with a slight S.W. wind. The outboard was used constantly, in fact they didn't put up the sails. At 08.15 we entered the Roach with the tide. At 09.00 with a recently published pilotage article in his hand the Master turned to port with the object of entering Yokesfleet. We went aground. The engine was put into reverse but with no success, with engine and tiller hard a port and Malcolm hanging from the shrouds we virtually unscrewed ourselves and found deeper water. With echo sounder having constant attention we made a cautious approach veering from side to side down the narrow channel. We successfully negotiated the passage between Potten Island and Foulness and entered Middleway. After this we went through Narrow Cuts between the islands of Havengore and Rushley and there before us was this beautiful new bridge. With such a marvellous construction it was inconceivable that it could have been built yet a little 21 footer couldn't get through. Their spirits were uplifted and so was the bridge. The Keeper waved to us from his lofty position, and I suspected there was a trace of a knowing grin on his face. Keep close to the north shore said the instruction, they did. Leave No.12 red can buoy to starboard said the guide. They did and went aground. Using the same technique i.e, going anti-clockwise with the Mate hanging over the side we got off and almost immediately went aground again. Having repeated this evolution a number of times we eventually reached No.10 buoy. You pass this no more than one boats length away. They did and went aground. This time we could not escape the clutches of the sands beneath us so as high tide was still an hour away they dropped anchor and opened the beer cans. High tide was 10.30 so with engine firing and anchor safely stowed we prepared to depart, but we didn't budge. They transferred weight aft, they transferred weight forward, they hung over the port side, they hung over the starboard side but all to no avail. We are now faced with being stuck for another twelve hours but suddenly the Master gets all authoritative.

"Right," he said, "we abort the trip." Now this was pretty obvious because we weren't getting anywhere. Then he said, "We've got to lighten ship, empty the water containers." You'll notice he didn't mention the beer and then, "One of us has got to go overboard, haven't you?" Common sense decrees that the heaviest should go, but common sense is not a quality the Master knows anything about.

Malcolm duly stripped off and went over the side. The effect was immediate – we floated off. "Don't come inboard yet," says the Skipper. "I'll tow you to deeper water."

Readers may well recall an earlier chapter where I mentioned how difficult it was to climb back aboard, so when the Master realised this he made himself a rope ladder which he tied to the grab rail as an insurance for his own safety whilst lone sailing. Well now was the time to use it and bring Malcolm in board, but he hadn't tied it correctly with the result that Malcolm's legs became entwined in the ladder as he slipped back into the sea. Now the Master is very proud of his creation and did not want to lose it, so ignoring the plight of his crew he made a grab for the ladder. He was of course unaware that Malcolm was so entrapped that if he lost one he'll lose the other. The Mate had by now lost confidence in the damned ladder and tried unsuccessfully to get aboard by using the guard rails. The Master however was insistent that his ladder be given a fair try out and so a half drowned shipmate came in board. It has been claimed in naval language crew going over the side can be put on a charge but all the skipper did was to offer him a stiff whisky. In actual fact Malcolm never got it and claimed it was his bottle anyway. If it was, then the Master had made a thorough job of polishing it off.

Order was eventually restored with the crew now decently clothed. The Bridge Keeper had obviously seen their antics and grinned at them as we made our return passage. The Master was most uneasy as he sensed this telepathic message saying, "I told you so."

With great care and caution we negotiated the creeks and cuts, the islands and the mudbanks. It was easy to see why this area should in days of old be a smugglers paradise.

By 11.30 we reached the Roach and for the first time the sails were set and a delightful sail dimmed the memory of this most unwelcome experience. By 13.00 we were back in Burnham Marina and being welcomed with the message: "We knew you wouldn't make it on neaps."

Already they are discussing making another attempt but this time on Beatrice. Poor Beatrice, poor Master, I wonder if he'll be the one forced to go over the side.

They did get to the Medway rally. They went by road.

BRIGHTLINGSEA – July 15/16th – organised by Colin Stonebridge

The good weather caused the majority of us to arrive in Brightlingsea on the Friday. Roaring Forty and Cambrian Lucy were in their home port; Kotuka II came from Woolverstone; Beatrice from Burnham and Baladin from Wallasea. Colin had arranged moorings for us, rafted up on harbour piles.

And then came the Medway boys - Ojala III (Tony Chamberlain), Moon Wisp (John Mason) and Free Bird, single-handed by Will Pretty who also contends with an artificial leg. He maintains he is the only member who can wring his leg out: it is constructed of specially moulded foam.

Roy Allgood and Liz came all the way from Brundall (Norwich) on Roy's Cobra, My Girl, and Pat and Bob McQueen on their lovely 27 ft. EEA Duchess of Portsmouth, from West Mersea. Imagine – eight Corribees and two bigger boats at an East Coast Rally! Then David and Kathy Bird flew in (sorry!). Will's wife drove up from Kent. Colin and Ann's son Peter, and his girlfriend, and Bob and Pat's son and daughter-in-law all joined us for dinner on the Saturday evening in the Swan Hotel. Twenty-two sat down in a room Colin had especially booked, so we all felt free and uninhibited. The food was excellent, the company superb and the stories – risqué. Colin gave an impromptu speech and it was close to 8 bells before we left.

We didn't have an official race, but with all these Corribees sailing in one direction up a river, one tended to develop a competitive edge. One of the Mudlark crews (Medway boys) went aground but before we had decided who would consume their dinner, they managed to get off. Back on the mooring, the Mudlarks produced some bottles of wine and in no time all the other skippers and crews had converged like bees round a honey pot…

Grateful thanks then, and a toast to our wives, sweethearts and lovers (it is permissible to have more than one!) who graciously or otherwise allow us to participate; to those shipmates who ferried us ashore and back throughout the weekend; to Robert Tucker for designing such a marvellous little boat; to the visitors by land who nobly supported us; to all the skippers and crews, especially the Mudlarks, and finally to Colin and Ann whose patience and perseverance over the years has seen this rally blossom and grow into the biggest attendance we have ever experienced. Finally the wonderful Corribee spirit of friendship and fun which is almost infectious... yes, I'll drink a special toast to that?

23
A Toast to the Ladies

Over the years Baladin has been a constant source of entertainment to me, however I am sure that those who have been forced to listen to our adventures do not share my enthusiasm, and indeed make a quick exit when they see me hove into view, it was therefore with some degree of relish that I accepted an invitation to toast the ladies at a firm's dinner. To have a captive audience such as this was an opportunity too good to miss.

The toast to the ladies went along these lines.

When I told my wife of this invitation her immediate response was, "Did you tell them you were a chauvinist?"

"No," I said.

To which she replied, "Well what do you know about women?"

"Well I've sort of been around."

"BEEN AROUND, been around, you told me I was the only girl you had taken out."

"Well- yes but you know you observe things."

"Observe what do you mean observe, are you becoming a dirty old man in your old age?"

It was obvious from our rather one sided conversation that I was losing out. After over 40 years of married life I should know better but it did get me thinking. What indeed did I know about women. I know the Almighty has formed them into the most exquisite shape known to mankind. Imagine if they had been square or conical. I will refrain from saying round but really the ladies' figures are always a constant delight to their male admirers, but I digress because there is so much I do not know. I don't know why a woman stops dead when she steps off an escalator, I don't understand how it is that they cannot manoeuvre a supermarket trolley, they block up the gangways and then at the checkout they wait until the cashier is finished before they start looking for their purse. Some years ago I decided to remedy this ignorance of mine and take unto myself a mistress.

It was at this stage in my dialogue I became conscious that the ladies in the audience froze. One could almost feel the hostility toward me. I endeavoured to carry on.

I wanted a young mistress, with appealing lines to her, elegant and shapely, a mistress who would not be demanding or possessive and who would not raise objections when I went home to my wife. Believe it or not there was such a being and I found her. We've been together for a number of years now during which time the only demands she has ever made is that I should once a year take her out of the water and scrub her bottom.

My audience changed. The hostile looks relaxed into waves of warm relief, and I was saved the embarrassment of making a hasty exit, but the point I wish to make regarding this event is that not only had Baladin given me the topic for the toast but had very carefully ensured that attention was directed at her. Her conceit and ego knows no bounds. She has all the wiles and ways of the fairer sex, she has all the qualities we adore and all the faults that we silently accept but please on no account tell her for I shall deny having said it.

24
Ensign Etiquette

"You," snapped the Chief Petty Officer instructor. "What does a commodore second-class have?"

"Two balls sir."

"So do you but that doesn't make you a bloody Commodore." Next man. "What does a commodore have?"

"A white fish tailed pennant with a red cross and one red ball sir."

"Correct."

That short exchange which occurred during my war time naval service sowed the seeds of resentment against commodores.

Such resentment followed me into civilian life but with the passage of time it slowly dimmed until that is a few years ago when "Baladin" and I were sailing out of Niewpoort in Belgium. Coming toward us was a fleet of motor launches all in line astern and all flying the red ensign.

On the first boat standing erect was the Commodore. His white cap with gold braid was at a jaunty angle. With one hand tucked into his gold buttoned blazer after the style of Napoleon and his white trousers it was obvious that he was out to impress.

One always gives a wave to a fellow compatriot but there was no response. Boat after boat went by without a flicker of acknowledgement. All eyes were dead ahead. Now I know that Baladin is toffee nosed, she's pretty and conceited, but she didn't deserve this off-handed treatment, so with a parting Churchillian gesture we expressed our farewells, but this incident revived my long held prejudices regarding commodores.

Some years later Dick Stace became Commodore of the Essex Marina Yacht Club, and you couldn't have a more charming and congenial character than Dick. In fact I was of the opinion that you couldn't be a commodore if you had the qualities I have attributed to Dick, but be that as it may I decided to subject Baladin to be a participant in the Sail Past.

Being one of the smallest boats we were the tail end Charlie. With a can of beer in one hand, the tiller in the other and a pipe of tobacco clenched firmly between my teeth we approached "Rhapsody" with a very dignified looking Dick standing on the bow. How could I ever have had doubts about commodores.

"Dip your ensign!" roared the Commodore. It took me by surprise because I jumped to attention, the boom hit me on the back of the neck, the pipe went flying, the can of beer clattered to the deck. I struggled to whip the ensign (staff and all) out of its socket and gave Dick a wave, meanwhile Baladin who had been left to her own devices had taken off at a tangent.

It was no surprise to find in the next issue of our magazine some kindly advice on etiquette. I do not like the word etiquette, it bespeaks of Victorian codes and mannerly conduct and when one is dressed in scruffy salt rimed trousers and a paint stained reefer jacket somehow the two do not seem compatible but the author of the article was not aware how deeply wounding his words had been to me.

I confided in a colleague the difficulties I was experiencing as a lone sailor trying to dip the ensign, but his only advice was to stick the flagstaff up my jackstay and waggle it about. I have no idea what he meant but somehow it sounded quite inelegant and even if I were to do as suggested I am sure Baladin would disown me. This of course brings me to the burgees. I love to see them flying and the more the merrier, but they say they should be flown from the starboard yard arm. I cannot do that, some idiot used the halyard for support with obvious results, so I fly mine from the port yard arm.

It has been suggested that I climb up the mast and fix it but I fear that would cause more problems than it would solve and sure as hell I'm not taking the mast down. It is true I advertised for a mini skirted young lady to shin up the mast for me but so far there have been no takers.

Etiquette decrees that burgees fly in some semblance of order but I tend to see their uses from a different point of view, for example when I fly the EMYC burgee that shows I am aboard. If I fly the EMYC and the COA (Corribee Owners Association) burgees that shows I am going upstream.

When I fly the EMYC (Essex Marina Yacht Club) and the RYA (Royal Yacht Association) burgee that shows I am going downstream. When I fly all three it means I don't know where the hell I'm going which then of course brings me to my fourth burgee. This is over fifty years old and is a relic of my youthful sea scouting days. When I fly that it indicates I do not wish to be disturbed as I am entertaining a member of the fair sex.

Fortunately my wife doesn't know about that one but alas it's never been used, it is still virginal if you get my meaning, but I digress. "Dip your ensign," says Dick but you will appreciate that this evolution is somewhat more difficult to perform than one would imagine so to all commodores past, present and future and wherever you might be please be assured that with all my misgivings, breaches of etiquette are not intended but are the result of overweight, over-age, over-indulgence and a petulant and precocious vessel!

EAST COAST RALLY
Friday, July 27th – Sunday, July 29th, 1990

Friday evening was spent within the confines of the Crouch Yacht Club to discuss the following day's activities. What other reason could there be? It was decided that the fleet would sail upstream to Wick Marina at North Fambridge where we would have lunch, all that is except Baladin whose long voyage had exhausted her Master so he was to join Malcolm Riggs and Ron Mepham aboard Beatrice. He was of course unaware at the time that he and Ron would be bruised, accused and mentally assaulted. They would be intimidated, castigated and sworn at, but it must have had some effect because they outstripped the other Corribees and fought neck and neck with Red Imp, Tony Chamberlain's Sadler 25.

On the way up we saw James and Jane Flint in their Corribee Dolce coming downstream from their mooring at North Fambridge to join us. They, whom we affectionately refer to as The Flintstones, turned round and joined the fleet. On arrival at North Fambridge the skipper of Beatrice, alias Altmark, sent Red Imp into Wick to get them stuck on the mud. Tony and Mary soon sussed that one out, and decided he couldn't get rid of the opposition that easy, so they exited pretty damn quick and joined Beatrice on the swing moorings pending the arrival of the rest of the fleet. We all relaxed and prepared lunch in the glorious sunshine.

Very soon Captain Riggs was preparing to depart, but he kept very quiet until 1445 when instructions were bellowed across the tranquil waters. "We depart 1500 and race back to Burnham." A flurry of activity was seen aboard the other vessels as their crews endeavoured to achieve in 15 minutes what we had been doing in 30.

At 1500 we slipped our moorings. Beatrice, who is very fast, carved her way through the fleet and took the lead. At one stage the skipper yelled at us to go about… as two yachts were bearing down on us, and even though we had right of way, it would cause pandemonium. We had 17' below us but the river bank was only 5 yards away, so the order was not obeyed as quickly as the captain would have wished, with the result we headed for the bank and then there was panic. The skipper tried to get the engine going while I rushed forward thinking my weight would be instrumental in grounding us before we hit the bank. Then, with the engine on, I could retire aft, and Beatrice would then shake herself free. I don't know what Ron was doing, but I suspect he had his hands in over his ears. We didn't actually hit the bank, nor did we touch bottom, but the current somehow caught our bows and poked us back again.

Now of course there had to be recriminations and an inquest. However, just as the captain was about to apportion blame, the crew, on the basis of a democratic vote, maintained the skipper must at all times be held to be responsible. We suffered for that – oh yes, we did suffer. The skipper started to sing to us but in tones that would have made Pavarotti sound like Des O'Connor. This went on until he saw Red Imp catching us up, and Poppy coming along like an express train. That was when the whips came out, and this lasted until he saw Poppy's sails flapping while we were still making good progress against wind and tide!

On Saturday evening, thirteen of us sat down to dinner in the Crouch Yacht Club, having been joined by Malcolm's wife, Maureen, and his daughter, Christine. Then, Graham Sharpley arrived, the owner of Cumbrian Lucy. It was a wonderful evening but for the second night running, it was nearly midnight when we left to take the path back along the sea wall to the marina.

Alas, Sunday came all too quickly. John Simons in Poppy left about 0800 to take advantage of the ebbing tide as they made their way back to the Medway. Martin and Janet Male left in Zeta soon afterwards to continue their holiday up the coast to the Blackwater. The rest of us had breakfast in the Yacht Club, and then Tony and Mary Chamberlain got ready to sail in Red Imp at 1100 to continue up the coast, with Cumbrian Lucy, who was going back to Brightlingsea.

Captain Riggs decided that he and his pressed gang should accompany them to the open sea. I think he wanted to show off his spinnaker but Red Imp beat him to it with a glorious display of colour which I ventured to suggest looked like Norah Batty's bloomers. We said our farewells and with a blustery wind, returned to the marina. With just Beatrice and Baladin left, it all seemed an anti-climax. We said cheerio to Ron and Baladin and I made our way back to Wallasea Marina.

25
The Future

It would be easy to say that this book records the adventures of a man and his boat. While that may be true it goes much deeper. Baladin is not an inanimate object, she has a will and a determination of her own which she exhibits most forcefully when the occasion warrants it. She can be flirtatious and at times downright obstructive, she can be petulant and coquettish, she can be proud and haughty and extremely conceited. She responds to my moods with understanding, she cannot however conceal her mocking ways at my ineptitude. Baladin does not of course make mistakes, but she can and does respond in a caring way when I fall asleep at the helm or get caught in bad weather. She'll give me a crack with the boom if I get above myself, and as you have already seen she will resort to the written word if she believes I may be tempted to embellish or exaggerate.

Our association is therefore a love story but with a difference. Age slowly creeps up on one so that you are not as nimble about ship as you may wish to be. The bones begin to creak, and the aches and pains of old age catch up so that it becomes necessary to think through every evolution you undertake to ensure that your sheets and tackle are in the right place at the right time. Age does not affect Baladin, her figure today is as trim as the day she was launched, her appearance is as attractive as it ever was. Time has stood still for her so that instead of growing old together she remains young and will never turn fat, grey and wrinkled.

I would like to believe we have been a team, joining together in overcoming difficulties, learning from one's mistakes of which there have been plenty. I do not accept that anyone can claim to know all there is to learn about sailing but I do claim with Baladin's assistance to have increased my own knowledge.

I have learned to study the winds and the tides and how one can use them to the best advantage. I have learned the need for patience and acceptance when there is no wind and the sails hang down in lifeless form. I know now that starting the engine is not an admission of failure but should be used to complement the sails and maybe wisely used to save losing the tide. I've learned to relax but not to dream, to be forever on the alert and never to take anything for granted. I've learned of the care and kindness of my fellow mariners. I've learned of the joy of sailing whether it be a glorious sunny day with a light breeze filling the sails, or gale force winds in heaving waters with a storm jib and fully reefed main. Each has its own particular form of enjoyment. The gentle lap of the water against the bows or the exhilarating feeling of the winds in the rigging and the gunwales awash both have their appeal.

The day will come as sure it must when Baladin and I will have to part. There will be no other boat, there never has, just Baladin and me. The thought fills me with foreboding but until that day arrives we will continue to sail together, enjoying each other's company. Baladin will still be instrumental in correcting me and I in turn will keep sweet talking her. We sail in the present and we think with affection of the past, the future is not ours to worry about.

BALADIN

Some time ago while writing about Baladin I concluded with the following paragraph.

"The day will come as sure it must when Baladin and I will have to part. There will be no other boat, there never has, just Baladin and me. The thought fills me with foreboding but until that day arrives we will continue to sail together enjoying each other's company. Baladin will still be instrumental in correcting me, and I in turn will keep sweet talking her. We sail in the present and we think with affection of the past. The future is not ours to worry about."

Alas that day has arrived and though my heart will always be with her, she now belongs to another. Baladin in these last few weeks played all sorts of tricks to deter potential buyers, and only eased up when a younger man came to see her, a man she can educate into her ways.

I told Baladin what I was proposing to do and though I know she did not like it, I believe she understood.

The day after the transfer I went to the marina just for a last farewell. Derek the new skipper said, "You've left your pipe rack behind."

Before I could say anything his pal John said, "If Geoff doesn't want it then leave it, it's all part of Baladin."

I could see the makings of an eternal triangle here because John too had fallen in love with her and was offering to buy her from Derek.

I left happy in the knowledge that she was in good hands and that her new master was already talking to her.

The next day I went down again, you know how it is, there was just a chance that I may be needed, but as I approached Baladin I saw my pipe rack lying on the pontoon. I just felt sad and prayed that Baladin was not aware of it.

Next year she will be going to Holland to live. She will be at home there, she knows the waters and the coastline; in the meantime she is now lying on the hard at Wallasea Island. I yearn to go and see her but resist the temptation. Wherever I am no matter what port or what country or what river or sea I will look out for her, and so I say to my beloved Baladin thank you and farewell and look after your new skipper as well as you looked after me.

I couldn't sleep at all last night, I lay awake tossing and turning and thinking of Baladin. I was tortured, my heart was breaking as I lay there fretting over the fact that she now belonged to another. Instead of increasing my hurt by dwelling on the lovely times we had together, I thought it would help were I to think of the other side of her character: the wilfulness, the stubbornness like the time I kept her out too long and she chucked the outboard over the side. I don't think I told you about that, I was too ashamed but she really did, she just got rid of it plus half of the engine bracket, and then with no wind and the tide against me she rammed the river bank. It didn't hurt her but it sure bruised my shins. It was dark too and I wasn't to know she was going to sabotage the navigation lights. It was nearly midnight when I got back to the marina. I tucked her up for the night and as I stood on the pontoon I gave a backward glance and then fell flat on my face. I'll swear to this day that I heard a quiet chuckle.

She is jealous, terribly jealous. I would never let her see me looking at another boat, and to be heard praising another vessel was almost suicidal. Malcolm Riggs found that out. I warned him. I said, "Malcolm don't talk about other boats in front of Baladin," but he didn't listen. One day I was leaning over the stern fiddling with the engine while Malcolm was extolling the praises of a passing yacht, suddenly Baladin hit him with the boom. I heard it, I heard the crack and when I saw Malcolm sitting down holding his head I thought he was play acting as a ploy to get at the whisky and then I looked at the boom, there was a dent in it. I'm telling you that there is a dent in the boom where she hit Malcolm on the head. She is vicious when she wants to be and uses that boom like a heavyweight boxer. She has a wicked upper cut and a damaging left jab but Malcolm had the full treatment. I've felt it many a time and it didn't have to be heavy weather. I've been becalmed, no wind and not a ripple on the water and she's swiped me. Once I got my feet wet when she gave me a back hander and all I was going to do was to start the engine. She never did like that engine.

There was the time we went aground, I think I told you, Malcolm was aboard and he had to go overboard to lighten the ship. We floated off the sand bank alright but when it came to bringing Malcolm inboard I tied a rope ladder to the grab rail. What happened? The knot came undone and I lost them both. I don't think she liked Malcolm. Come to think of it I don't think she liked the rope ladder either.

Do you remember the three young ladies, beautiful girls that looked like fashion models when we set sail from the marina but three hours later with a lovely sunny day they came back soaking wet with their clothes sticking to their bodies. Their hair hung in long dank rat tails, while streaks of mascara ran down cold shivering cheeks. Baladin did that, and she achieved her object because those girls never came back again.

You remember the hurricane in October 1987, you remember I sent her down to Somerset to be repaired by Newbridge. It's a funny thing but shortly after that they went bankrupt. Now I'm not saying anything but if she heard anyone making a disparaging remark, well work it out for yourself.

She had another trick, baton flicking. You'd be sitting at the helm at peace with the world and suddenly a sail baton would fly past your ear. You would then recall that you hadn't spoken to her for half an hour so you have to apologise.

Have you seen the main sheet traveller fly across the boat and smash the end stoppers so that the main sheet flapped uncontrollably and out of reach? Baladin could do that and in the passage of time she refined it so that she knocked me off balance with the boom, I would fall backwards onto the mainsheet release and away would go the main. She got two with one blow with that little trick.

Do you remember the time she attacked that Swedish merchant ship? I thought she had gone mad and it wasn't as if she had one go, she kept on going back like a young terrier. Baladin was alright she wasn't hurt, the merchant ship got scratched but what about me? Baladin goes in for the final assault on his stern, but who got the garbage chucked over him? Me bloody me and all just because she didn't like foreign ships in our rivers.

There's that cleat on the forecastle, the one that lies amidships, she is lethal with that. She waits until it is really rough, the sort of weather when you have to crawl forward and lie on your stomach to take the jib down. Baladin loved that and with every wave she would ram it into your belly. She has an evil sense of humour.

One day I thought I would get her exorcised and then thought better of it for as sure as hell (if that is the appropriate expression) she'd have knocked the priest overboard.

There is so much more I could tell you but I won't bore you further, I've got it out of my system and I feel a lot better for it, I only hope that I don't break my leg taking this to the post box.

Thanks for listening but please let no one read this in front of Baladin.

Sweet Dreams.